CARLSBAD CAVERNS

NATIONAL PARK

WORLDS OF WONDER

by Candace Crane

Dedicated to the spirit of my beloved El Lobo.
May you regain all your land.

Acknowledgments

A book is the child of many people who believe in it. The author gets her name on the cover for birthing the words, but it belongs equally to those who have been behind the scenes, contributing to it in their various ways. Without the following, *Worlds of Wonder* would not exist.

They are the many, many people, too numerous to name, who granted me interviews, led me through the park, and made themselves available to answer questions all along the way. They were so generous with their time and help. In particular, mammalogist Dr. Ken Geluso gave me significant interview time, invaluable manuscript reviews, and, most importantly, encouragement during the rough spots that every book goes through on its way to being born. Dale Pate, cave resource manager of Carlsbad Caverns National Park, also extended his support beyond the call of duty. During the final stage of manuscript development, Dale's commitment to seeing the book completed was like a sturdy rope pulling me up a last cliff to the mountaintop. They are the friends — both human and animal — who gave me steady, often silent, support through all my frustrations, impatience, general rantings, and threats about giving up. Leading the list are my ex-husband and friend, Ted Judd; my editor at *Animals* magazine, Joni Praded; and my best compadre, Ken Strom. Kelly Dickson, Jack Hovingh, Bob Campbell, and Bethann Dussau are others who made a real difference. My horse, Fire, magically renewed and rebalanced me after long workdays. My dogs, Tuppence and Montana, brought levity to the project, smiling and tail-wagging through it all. My turtles, TG and Blossom, reminded me of the wisdom in sitting still until the answer comes.

They are the production team: Melinda Lang, who captured my heart's intent in her sensitive design, making the book one whole, and the Impact Photographics group, whose steady hand and commitment to high quality gave the book visual integrity. They are my publisher and friend, Rick LoBello; his clients at the National Park Service, Superintendent Frank Deckert and Chief of Interpretation Ed Greene; and Rick's entire board of directors. When the manuscript was delayed because of my breast cancer, you all stuck by me. You voted to believe in me.

They are my rock, Lord, and healer, Jesus Christ. He extended grace to me through those I've named here and others. I praise him for giving me the eyes to see the beauty of the natural world, the heart to care about it, and the talent to share it with others.

Thank you all.

Candace Crane, March, 2000

Table of Contents

The Creation

chapter one

*"So the story really gets going about 320
million years ago, when Africa slammed
into North America," I said to my
compadre, Ken Strom.
"Yeah, it was no small fender-bender,"
he replied, gazing thoughtfully at the
landscape below.
From where we stood on the ridge,
which was an ancient limestone reef,
southeast New Mexico lay spread below
us like a faded gray-green quilt. Straight
ahead lay the wide, white expanse of a
sea bed, once filled with deep primal
waters and capped with large waves.
To our right, the reef, now uplifted as the
rugged Guadalupe Mountains, curved
into the distance, tracing the old sea's
shoreline. We were here at Carlsbad
Caverns National Park for a week to discover the story behind this landscape. As
I took it all in, the eons seemed to slip
away and I envisioned what it must
have been like when it was being born.*

*Prehistoric waters were home to a wide and
colorful array of coral-reef creatures, such as
fan-like bryozoans, vase-shaped sponges,
feathery sea lilies, and horn corals.*

Photo credit—NPS

The two land masses, one holding the future North America, the
other the future Africa, had been sliding toward one another for
awhile. When they finally collided, it was with such force that the
edges of both continents crumpled like car fenders. The shock
buckled land well into the interior of North America, splitting in two
a huge, low-lying basin that would someday encompass southeast
New Mexico and west Texas.

The basin had already been in existence for 500 million years,
and had, at various times, held seas. In them, life had evolved. Fish,
sharks, and an amazing array of small invertebrates had appeared.
They flourished near the surface, and when they died, they sank.
Cemented together by calcium carbonate in the water, they eventually became thin beds of limestone. Rivers from distant mountains
carried sediment into the sea, creating layers of sandstone between
the limestone.

Now waters flowed again into the basin, creating two seas in the
broken halves. The one of our interest, someday to be called the
Delaware Sea, was 150 miles long, 75 miles wide, and two thousand
feet deep. It was connected to the open Permian Ocean by a narrow
channel that kept the waters circulating.

About 260 million years ago, conditions were such that a reef
began growing in this sea a half-mile out from the shore. Blue-green
algae, fan-like colonies of bryozoans, vase-like sponges, and clam-
like brachiopods were the major players. Lesser actors included
feathery sea lilies, trumpet-like horn corals, and spiralled nautiloids.
When they died, their calcium carbonate shells were broken up by
waves and rocks until they formed a limey sediment. More calcium
carbonate, from the water and certain of the reef-builders themselves, cemented this mass together, building, inch by inch, a
limestone reef. Such a special stone is limestone, formed not just
by inorganic chemistry, but by living things!

In back of the reef, a shoal rose, creating a lagoon and tidal flats
behind it. Sometimes the shoal was slightly submerged; sometimes
it rose above the water to form a line of low islands. Wetting and
drying over thousands of years caused the earth here to buckle and

Photo credit—NPS

crease, forming tepee-looking structures that defined the shore.

In the warm, shallow lagoon, evaporation created a highly salty environment where only a few creatures, such as clams and snails, could survive. Here the sea deposited limestone in layers. From bottom to top, they would come to be called the Queen, Seven Rivers, Yates, and Tansill formations. Behind the lagoon, the tidal flats stretched for dozens of miles. Alluvial plains from faraway mountains swept silt and sand onto them, which became other rocks.

About 260 million years ago, a horseshoe-shaped limestone reef began forming in the sea that covered southeast New Mexico. It would one day be known as the Capitan Reef and hold some of the world's most magnificent caves.

Over millennia the reef grew. Its growth was seaward most of the time, but sometimes it grew so far out it could not support itself. Then, house-sized boulders would break off and tumble into the basin, forming a steep talus slope. The reef would then build upward, on top of this slope. In this way, first the narrow Goat Seep Reef, and then the wider Capitan Reef, were built. For 10 million years the Capitan built, until it had formed a 400-mile horseshoe around the sea two to three miles wide and almost two thousand feet high.

Many times over these eons, gravity and mountain-building movements from far away caused the reef to slump toward the basin and crack at the contact with its talus slope. In this process, it also pulled away from the lagoon, opening fissures and fractures. They cut vertically through the limestone and sandstone, some perpendicular and some parallel to the reef. Without these humble cracks, the parkland's subsequent history would have taken a far different turn.

Over time, the circulation of water from the ocean lessened — for what reason we do not know for certain — until the Delaware Sea began to evaporate. As it did, the remaining water grew much too salty for the reef-building creatures. They began to die out, and the reef ceased growing. Gradually, salts, sand, and silt filled the basin and then covered the reef. By 250 million years ago, no sign was left of the great sea and reef.

Perhaps it was just as well. All over the earth, one of the greatest extinctions of all time was occurring. Ninety percent of all species were vanishing, including almost all the reef-builders. The force of life would not be curtailed, however. While the sea was being buried, terrestrial reptiles had been developing and dinosaurs were about to appear.

In the subtropical climate of the parkland, the earliest "karstification" was occurring, a process that would shape a land of caves. The process went like this: when the abundant rain soaked into the earth, it picked up carbon dioxide from the dead plants and animals there, turning into a weak carbonic acid. As this acid seeped into the fissures between the old reef and lagoon, it ate away the limestone, enlarging the cracks into small caves. Over time these collapsed and filled with clay and limestone rock fragments. But like the fissures that parented them, they were crucial to our story because they created porous places where water, or even oil, could rest. In this way, they were determining where future caves developed.

Over the next hundred million years, dinosaurs and then mammals rose to prominence. Geological movements finally caused the open sea to inundate the continent, and it became a series of islands. Part of the Delaware Basin held a sea again, which geologists would call the Comanchean Sea.

As far as 20,000 feet under this sea lay vast reserves of oil and gas that encompassed the whole region. Since even before the days of the Delaware Sea, sediments had been burying plants and animals when they died. As the weight of these sediments on the organic matter increased, so did the temperature, cooking the organic matter and converting it to oil and gas. This was a continuous process, occurring in different layers of rock in the parkland at different times. Certain bacteria in this brine of oxygen-free saltwater and oil used the hydrocarbons, creating hydrogen sulfide gas in the process. Like the tiny cracks in the rock, these tiny creatures are important in our story.

Eighty million years ago, two plates of the earth's crust collided rather rapidly, buckling the entire western portion of the land mass that would become the U.S. The collision raised the whole Rocky Mountain region, from the future Wyoming to the future New Mexico. In the parkland, the old reef and sea basin was lifted 1,300 feet above sea level and tilted eastward.

Meanwhile, underground, the movement of water through the reef's limestone enlarged the old fissures and joints in the reef into what geologists would call "spongework." These little caves were small, with a random pattern of chambers that sometimes did, sometimes didn't, connect. Like the fissure caves before them, they set the scene for the drama that lay ahead.

Now that the reef was raised, the sediments that had been deposited on top of it over millions of years began to erode away. Time passed. The uplift of the Rockies subsided. The climate cooled as the continents drifted toward their present positions. Erosion reduced the reef to flattened, low-lying plains. Meandering streams crossed the area, cutting deep valleys and canyons. While this was happening the dinosaurs abruptly became extinct 65 million years ago.

Mammals quickly took center stage and grew into their new starring roles, diversifying and spreading. By 40 million years ago, small canids, bats, and the horse — albeit in a humble fox-sized, forest-dwelling version — had appeared.

At this time, magma deep inside the earth in the southern Rockies began to rumble and spurt, signalling more changes in our parkland. Volcanic domes arose over the landscape. Then faulting began to pull the entire region apart. Deep basins sank and adjacent areas were pushed up. Mountains rose from New Mexico into Utah and Nevada. In this process, the future parkland's mountains formed a steep arch along the fault. Underground, the cooling of thermal waters lined the spongework caves with what would be known as "thermal spar" — large calcite crystals.

Twenty million years ago, more earth movements broke the arched region apart, and a great series of almost vertical uplifts pushed our deeply carved reef nearly nine thousand feet up into the sky of the future Texas. From there it ran northeast, sloping gently down to four thousand feet, where it disappeared underground. These, finally, were the Guadalupe Mountains, spectacular with their deep canyons and flat ridge tops from the old, eroded plain.

Twenty million years ago, mountain building began pushing the Capitan Reef up into the air, creating the Guadalupe Mountains. Underground, fresh water from the water table flowed into the reef's cracks and cavities. As uplift continued, hydrogen-sulfide-rich brine from oil-bearing rocks traveled into the reef and mixed with the fresh water, creating sulfuric acid that began carving out the Guadalupes' big, glorious caves.

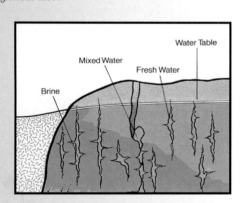

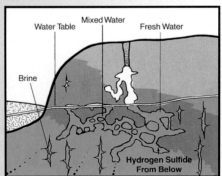

During this uplift, which lasted for 18 million years, fresh water was allowed to flow into the reef, creating an aquifer. The water sought the easiest channels, filling the cracks, joints, and cavities of the reef: the old fissure and spongework caves.

Meanwhile, the hydrocarbons from the oil-bearing rocks of the Delaware basin began moving upward into the reef. Scientists are not certain what triggered their movement — possibly mountain building, possibly down-cutting of the river that would someday be called the Pecos, possibly both. However it happened, about 12 million years ago the brine reached the level of the aquifer and shot into the fresh water in tremendous bursts. When the brine's hydrogen sulfide gas mixed with the oxygen-rich fresh water, it was oxidized to sulfuric acid, which began carving out of the reef the big, glorious caves of the Guadalupes. Two of them, in the Capitan Reef, would become the treasures known as Carlsbad Cavern and Lechuguilla Cave.

As the mountains continued lifting and the water of the aquifer sought the lowest routes through the reef, this mixing zone moved progressively lower. Thus, the first caves to be created were high in the mountains. It was not until six million years ago that work began on the Cavern, as well as Lechuguilla.

The mountains that were raised had spectacular, deeply carved canyons and flat ridgetops created by erosion of the soft reef limestone over millennia. El Capitan Peak in Guadalupe Mountains National Park, overlooking the old sea basin, stands as a silent witness to the drama.

Photo credit—Laurence Parent

Historical Dates

1400   Mescalero Apaches come to the Guadalupe Mountains area.

1536   Cabeza de Vaca is the first of the Spanish explorers to cross southeastern New Mexico.

1745   Padre Juan Miguel Menchero maps the area of present day Carlsbad.

1849   Numerous expeditions cross this area recently acquired by the United States.

1850   September 9, New Mexico becomes a Territory.

1855   The U. S. Army begins scouting the Guadalupes for Mescalero Apache raiders.

1858   The route of the Butterfield Overland Mail runs through the Guadalupe Mountains. A stage station is established at Pine Springs.

1869   Lieutenant Howard B. Cushing mounts a punitive expedition from Fort Stanton against Mescalero raiders in the Guadalupes.

1878   The Tenth Cavalry (nicknamed the "Buffalo Soldiers") establishes a permanent camp in the Guadalupe Mountains.

1881   Henry Harrison arrives from Indiana and homesteads at Rattlesnake Springs. Cavalry patrols use his farm as a point of supply during the 1880s.

1882   William C. Sublett finds gold nuggets in the Guadalupe Mountains eight to twelve miles from Pine Springs.

       July 11, Jim White, future explorer of Carlsbad Cavern, is born in Mason County, Texas.

1888   Former sheriff Pat Garrett and promoter Charles Greene join with Charles Eddy to create a system of canals and flumes for diversion of water to their properties.

1889   October 6, The first school in Eddy opens on South Main with 35 pupils.

1891   The first railroad train arrives in Eddy on the newly completed line from Pecos, Texas.

1892   Jim White's family settles at Lone Tree, a ranching community eight miles east of Eddy.

1894   By October, the railroad is complete from Eddy to Roswell, NM.

1898   The first hospital and library are started in Eddy.

       Rock in main corridor inscribed "J White" and "1898" suggests that White probably entered the cavern for the first time in 1898.

1903 to 1923 Main period of guano mining at the Cavern.

1906   June 8, The Antiquities Act gives the President power to proclaim national monuments and also prohibits excavation or appropriation of antiquities on federal lands.

1912   January 6, New Mexico becomes a state, 62 years after becoming a Territory.

1916   August 25, Congress establishes the National Park Service.

Since the chemicals and processes creating these Guadalupe caves were different than those creating most others, they would have an unusual — and dramatic — character. Huge rooms in random patterns; unpredictable passageways that end abruptly; pits and chimneys connecting the levels...these were the signatures of our caves.

At first, the Cavern was a nondescript maze of tiny water-filled passageways and solution pockets, a honeycomb with corridors. But as the acid ate away tight joints, ever more water was allowed through, creating large trunk passages. Water from these passages ascended toward outlets on the surface, creating sloping hallways and smooth, curved ceilings. As the level of the water table lowered over the next two million years, the primary worksites shifted: first the Natural Entrance, then Bat Cave, then the Kings Palace area, and finally Lake of the Clouds, over one thousand feet underground. This would be the deepest place humans would discover in Carlsbad Cavern in the 20th century, and even then, underneath their feet, the acid would be carving out more passages in the dark.

The huge rooms at each of the levels formed when the water table paused and intense mixing of fresh water with sulfuric acid could go on in one place for a time. Gas gushed out at a place that would one day be called the Bottomless Pit, producing acid that dissolved out the Big Room. Gas injecting into Lower Cave formed the dome at Top of the Cross. And so it went, over the eons.

While the caves were being carved out, mammals were flourishing on the surface of the parkland. Camels, jaguars, and four-horned antelopes evolved. The horse began as a fawn-sized forest animal, finally blossoming, about two million years ago, into modern *Equus*. It and other mammals began to grow larger and move between continents over land bridges. Over the next 1.5 million years or so, mammals wandered into this area from Eurasia including the giant *Bison antiquus*; the shrub ox, short-haired relative of the musk ox; the Columbian mammoth; the caribou; gray wolf; and mountain sheep. From Africa would come the lion, and from South America, the ground sloth.

Photo credit—Russ Finley

Sulfuric acid carved the Guadalupe caves with an unusual and dramatic character. Huge rooms — such as the Big Room shown here — unpredictable passages, large trunk passages, deep pits, and curved ceilings were their signatures.

As their migrations began, glaciers in the far north began the first of at least 18 advances and retreats that set the rhythm for life until ten thousand years ago. When they advanced, the climate would grow cooler and moister, even in areas far from the ice, as the parkland was, and plants and animals would shift south. At these times, low elevations in the park were spread with lush, open grasslands, scattered stands of pines and oaks, lakes, and streams. The high mountains grew dense forests of pine and spruce. Summers were cool and winters mild. During glacial retreats, the climate grew warmer and drier. Animals and plants moved north, out of the parkland, and into its higher elevations.

As the glacial rhythms continued, so did the lowering of the water table. As the water drained from areas of the Cavern, their enlargement ceased. Sometimes this happened before the limestone had completely dissolved. Such areas were left unfinished, looking much like Swiss cheese. Cavers would later call this formation "boneyard." In the Big Room, when water no longer buoyed up loose sections of reef, they thundered to the floor as "breakdown." Water that had been held in the rock and water from the surface came in through every pore and fissure, picking up dissolved limestone on the way. When the water hit the air, chemical changes caused it to release the limestone, depositing it, mostly as calcite.

With this calcite as a master tool, around 800,000 years ago the water began to decorate with a multitude of different formations. It dripped, forming stalactites and stalagmites. It flowed, creating flowstone. It evaporated, making popcorn, balloons, aragonite needles, and rimstone dams. It seeped out small pores forming spaghetti-like helictites, which

seem to defy gravity. It pooled, forming clouds and lily pads. As a sculptor works with many tools, so the water used the porosity of the rock, the minerals in the water, the joints through which it flowed, the rate at which it flowed, the changing temperature of the cave, even the movement of the air to create surprising variations. Sometimes acids in the soil or trace minerals in the water brought in color: black from manganese, reds from iron, browns and oranges from organic acids.

As the climate on the surface changed with the rhythm of the glaciers, the decorating project in the Cavern followed suit. During glacial retreats, when conditions were rather dry, work slowed or stopped,

Photo credit—NPS

Around 800,000 years ago, water began to decorate Carlsbad Caverns with a multitude of different formations. In what would be known as the Kings Palace, decorating reached mind-boggling levels. Its Papoose Room, shown here, would be called the most highly decorated room in the cave.

and deposits were milky. When the glaciers advanced, bringing more rain above and more moisture below, formations would grow, with lustrous surfaces and vibrant color. The dampest period, from 600,000 to 500,000 years ago, must have seen a great fog hanging in the Cavern all the time and decorating proceeding at a furious rate. Bat Cave entrance may have opened at this time.

Probably during another wet period, crickets, millipedes, and other invertebrates sought shelter in the Cavern and began to shape a cave ecosystem. It would be simple, dark, little changing, with little food to offer, but the creatures would adapt. In fact, some would adapt so well it would be impossible for their kind to return to the surface to live.

1918 — First photographs in the Cavern's Scenic Rooms and Big Room taken by Ray V. Davis. His photographs stimulate interest in the Cavern. His photos appear in the *New York Times* in 1923.

1923 — April 6, Robert Holley, General Land Office, surveys and maps cave, guided by Jim White and photographed by Ray Davis of Carlsbad. May 8, Holley recommends establishment as a national monument.

August 6, Major Richard Burgess, prominent El Paso lawyer, begins campaign to make the Cavern a national monument. Proposes construction of a tunnel from the plains into the cavern to reduce difficulty of access. Tunnel supported by NPS Director Mather until huge cost makes it impractical.

September 19, Dr. Willis T. Lee first explores the Cavern and recommends national park status. Lee's article appears in February 1924 *National Geographic* magazine.

October 25, President Calvin "Silent Cal" Coolidge speaks up and proclaims Carlsbad Cave National Monument.

1923 to 1927, W.F. McIlvain serves as first custodian (superintendent), overseeing first trails, stairs, lights. He supervises Jim White, works with Willis T. Lee, coordinates with city officials, including Chamber of Commerce, and makes $12/year.

1924 — March 20 to September 15, Dr. Willis T. Lee, sponsored by National Geographic Society and assisted by Jim White, extensively explores Cavern. NPS Director Mather visits in April.

1925 — Staircase from Natural Entrance to Bat Cave is installed, eliminating use of guano bucket to enter cave. Donated by Carlsbad Chamber of Commerce.

September, Willis T. Lee's second *National Geographic* article, detailing his second visit, is published.

1926 — First trail is finished by NPS, dirt path and wooden stairways through Main Corridor, King's Palace, Queen's Chamber, and 3/4 of Big Room. First electric lighting system via Main Corridor and King's Palace is installed.

1927 — May 16, Col. (an honorary title)Thomas Boles enters on duty as first superintendent. Serves until 1946. At retirement Boles notes that he administered (spent) approximately $3 million in appropriated park funds during his tenure and collected about $3.5 million in fees during the same period.

Trail past Bottomless Pit opens. School for employees' children established in park. The Cavern Supply Company is established as the park concessioner. Fees to enter caves: $2.00 per person.

Soon afterward, in geological terms, erosion of the reef also exposed the large Natural Entrance, establishing the Cavern's breathing cycle and allowing animals to wander in. About 112,000 years ago, an animal did enter and die there, leaving us the earliest record we have of an animal in a Guadalupe cave. It was a Shasta ground sloth, a big, shaggy, grizzly-bear looking animal about seven feet long. Mostly an open-country animal, it browsed on almost any vegetation it could stuff in its mouth. It used caves routinely and may have seasonally moved up and down in elevation.

Not long afterward, 100,000 years ago, the Ice Age most familiar to us from movies began. By now, the whole cast of Pleistocene mammals had wandered into the area to join the sloth: the dire wolf, North American lion, saber-toothed cat, short-faced bear, mammoth, four-horned antelope, camel, and of course, the horse. By 35,000 years ago, many of them were using the Guadalupe caves. About this time, mega-bats, the Ice Age version of free-tailed bats, found Slaughter Canyon Cave and began roosting and raising babies there. They may have

Photo credit—NPS

The giant ground sloth, a seven-foot shaggy bear-like animal from South America, was among the large prehistoric mammals that lived in the area of the park a hundred thousand years ago.

found and started to use other caves in our future park as well, but we have no record of that.

By at least 13,000 years ago, humans had arrived, and some were living in small caves in the Guadalupe Mountains. One such cave in the park shows remnants of occupation. Watching the rising sun from the entrance, the humans may have put a log on their hearth and breakfasted on mammoth. They may have added juniper berries, or yucca flowers, or acorns, depending on the season. When they left the cave, they may have covered

their smoldering hearth with twigs and leaves. Later, the dire wolf that died here may have entered because it was injured, driven from its pack, and was attracted by the smell of mammoth. Perhaps it took its last meal from the humans' leavings. If something like this did happen, accounting for the remains here, it would be one of the earliest records of humans in the New World.

By 11,000 years ago nomadic Clovis people followed their food sources throughout what would become eastern New Mexico. They hunted both the Columbian mammoth and *Bison antiquus*, as well as horses, camels, and smaller animals like jackrabbits. Because they enjoyed a warm climate with a long growing season, plants were probably also important food, especially since the large mammals moved so much that hunting on foot was difficult. Clovis people camped on the parkland's open grasslands near lakes and in its caves overlooking streams.

By 10,500 years ago, the climate began to change. Winter rains dwindled, and summers grew warmer. In response, the trees of the low elevations began to withdraw. Grasses and desert scrub moved in to take their place. Vegetation on the whole decreased. With less to eat, mammals declined in numbers or grew smaller. *Bison antiquus*, with its three-foot spread of horns, began to downsize in the direction of the modern bison.

By this time, the Folsom people had replaced the Clovis. They followed the same food and living pattern but focused on hunting bison instead of the disappearing mammoth. The bison had dispersed into small herds, which required the Folsom people to be highly mobile to be successful in hunting. Their craftsmen fashioned exquisitely finished, fluted stone points for hunting. These were lashed to a lance for close-up killing and projected with an atlatl — a spearthrower — for long-distance hunting.

The pace of change now quickened. By the time the final glaciation ended 10,000 years ago, the continent's mega-mammals had all become extinct. The horse, camel, and North American lion, for reasons still a mystery, had left the native home they were so well adapted to and settled on other continents. Moist periods had grown shorter; the climate warmer and drier. By eight thousand years ago, the oak-pine woodland was gone from lower elevations in the parkland, and in its place were desert grasslands. Most of the lakes had dried up. Game had become scarce. Bison now gathered in large, migratory herds, forcing people to change the way they hunted. They developed the mass-kill technique of driving bison over cliffs and the idea of specialized campsites.

Then, about seven thousand years ago, the bison migrated north, to return several thousand years later. The people may have followed them, since we have no record of either from the parkland for this long period of time. Happily, this was not our story's end. Only an interlude for life to catch its breath.

As early as 13,000 years ago, small bands of humans inhabited the Guadalupe Mountains. They migrated with their food sources, hunting large game with stone-pointed spears, gathering plants in season, and seeking shelter in the many caves of the region. About seven thousand years ago, they seemed to disappear from the region.

Photo credit—NPS/Dave Bunnell

1927	June 23, First wedding ceremony is held in cave, performed at Rock of Ages.
1928	February, Charlie White (no relation to Jim) homesteads 120 acres at Walnut Canyon, the future White's City.
	May 16, Cavern Supply Company begins serving lunches in cave.
	June, Trail from top of Appetite Hill to lunchroom opens.
	November, Electric lighting in Big Room completed. Guides carry lanterns for emergencies only.
1929	March, Tunnel through Devil's Den is completed and opened.
	May, First stone quarters completed.
	June 26, Jim White resigns due to failing health.
	June, Green Lake Room and King's Palace connected by tunnel and trail constructed.
	July 27, First Rock of Ages ceremony held.
	September, First bat flight program is presented.
	November, Nature trail opens to public.
1930	March, Trail from Lower Cave Overlook to Top of the Cross opens, eliminating need to double back to the Totem Pole during tours.
	February 18, Lake of the Clouds is discovered.
	February 20, Writer Frank Ernest Nicholson with 14 assistants arrives to explore the Cavern.
	April 16, Tunnel at entrance is completed; staircase to Bat Cave area is abandoned.
	May 14, Congress designates Carlsbad Caverns National Park.
1931	August, Elevator shaft is completed.
	November, First elevator is installed.
1932	Lights are installed in Green Lake and Papoose Rooms, completing original electric lighting system.
	June, First female guides employed.
	July 3, Tunnel between Papoose Room and King's Palace is completed and opens, thereby completing entire cave trail system.
1934	April 7, 2,871 people accompany the 10:30 a.m. guided tour, making this the largest single guided tour through the Cavern to date.
1935	June 24, Rattlesnake Springs replaces Oak Springs as park water source.
1937	February 9, Jim White begins selling his book (ghostwritten by Frank Ernest Nicholson) in the cave.
	July, Tom Tucker discovers Slaughter Canyon Cave (New Cave).
	September 28, Park receives 1 millionth visitor.

The Discovery

Our little group stood around the first mescal plant of the season to be harvested, waiting for Joey and Nathaniel, the Mescalero Apache medicine men, to give the blessing. This was an important harvest, for not only would it feed the public in an upcoming cele- bration in Carlsbad, but the first plants would go to the feastgivers — 30 girls of the tribe who were becoming women and would be honored with their own feast. The spring morning here on this ranch near Carlsbad Cavern was already hot, and the Guadalupes were taking on the smoky look that comes from heat. I looked around the circle at the mixture of people: Indian and Anglo, all ages, all sizes, talking and laughing with each other as if we'd been friends for years. Suddenly Nathaniel raised his hand for quiet and began the ceremony. He spoke of the mescal as a sacred gift to his people, given centuries ago to sustain them in all times, and how harvesting it together would bring unity among us. Then Joey performed the blessings, the harvesting stick was put to the base of the plant, and the first feastgiver pounded the stick with a sledgehammer until the mescal head fell loose from its roots. The harvest was now officially open, and we scattered over the range to get to work.

Three thousand years ago humans reappeared in the Guadalupes. Known as Archaic hunter-gatherers, they lived in cave entrances and depended mainly on plant foods but also hunted rabbits with snares and sometimes big game with stone-pointed spears. They cooked over rock hearths, and when the rocks cracked from heat, they'd push the pieces out around the fire and rebuild the hearth. Gradually, a circular midden ring of broken rock, wood ash, and food refuse built up. They made tools of stone and baskets of yucca, and in spare moments, they played with their pet dogs and decorated lances.

Dramatic changes were in store for them. Around 1300 AD, bands of Athapascans in Canada began to migrate south along the Rockies. When they reached the American Southwest around 1500, they spread throughout the region, and their culture grew to dominance over the Archaic. The new people would be called Apaches by the Spanish.

Over time, the subgroup that settled in the rugged mountains and dry plains of southeast New Mexico learned to be at home in their tough land. At first with only their feet and dogs, later with horses, they moved through the country constantly, following the ripening food. They learned to prepare over 125 wild plants, but their staple was mescal, which they gathered by the ton, baked in pits, and stored. The Spanish named them "mescal makers" — Mescalero.

From first contact with the Spanish in the 1500s, all Apache groups had trouble — both sides raided each other constantly. By the early 1700s, Comanches pushed into the territory, increasing pressure on the Apaches and making raiding for food and horses part of their way. Spain and Mexico campaigned against them, but the Apaches were desert-tough and could endure. They could go without water for days and fight guerrilla style, splitting and scattering, van- ishing into mountains, refusing to be brought to bay.

In the 1840s the Americans came. They would finally undo the Apaches, though it would be their most difficult Indian campaign. Soon after the Southwest Territory was annexed, it was opened by a trail that started in St. Louis, passed near the Cavern, and continued

Around 1500, the Mescalero Apache people settled in the region. Their history teaches that during the annual harvest of the mescal plant, spirit beings came to help. They gave the tribe the dance of the mountain gods as a blessing for every endeavor.

Photo credit—Friends of The Living Desert

to the California gold fields. As traffic picked up along it, Apache raids increased, too, and Ft. Davis was established in 1852 to quiet them. Raids by both sides were followed by many attempts at peace, which were always broken. In the late 1850s, John Butterfield tied the country together via stage, his Butterfield Overland Mail carrying mail and passengers over Guadalupe Pass. With this new traffic, settlers arriving, and the government-subsidized decimation of the buffalo, conflict reached a crescendo, and by the late 1860s the Army was acting to carry out Apache removal.

In 1870 the Buffalo Soldiers of the 9th and 10th cavalries and 24th and 25th infantries were sent from Ft. Davis to the Guadalupes, the roughest Mescalero stronghold. These black soldiers, many of them former slaves and Civil War veterans, were among the Army's toughest — a good match for the Apache. In their first strike in 1870, they confiscated 10 tons of mescal, leaving the Mescalero without food for the winter. In 1875 the tribe finally entered their reservation, but western Apaches continued fighting under Victorio.

Victorio's small band of warriors ran the cavalry ragged for two more years before the Buffalo Soldiers, in a brilliant move, kept him from water and pushed him into Mexico, where Mexican troops killed him. Surrender came shortly, after which the Army's general ordered retribution on the Apaches. As part of it, the peaceful reservation Mescalero were herded into a horse corral to live until they became so ill they had to be pulled out.

Now the land was safe for settlers. In 1880 Henry Harrison homesteaded at Rattlesnake Springs. For his hay and orchards he built an irrigation system, diverting water from the spring for the first time. In 1888 Carlsbad became a town.

The yawning Cavern 26 miles away had been known about for years. But credit for most of the early exploration goes to James Larkin White, a Texas-born cowboy. As White told his story, he was mending fences one day around 1900 when he came upon "the great hole under long slabs of yellow and gray stone." White looked eagerly into the darkness, then returned to work, but he could not forget the cave. A few days later, he returned to the mouth of the cave and, making a ladder of sticks, rope and wire, entered the cave carrying only a coal-oil lantern. He found the bat section of the cave and went as far as what he'd soon name Devil's Spring. His imagination about what lay beyond his dim lantern light captured him, and he resolved to see all of the cave he could reach.

1938	February 16, Discovery of Slaughter Canyon Cave (New Cave) is announced to public.
	July 1, Civilian Conservation Corps (CCC) camp is established at Rattlesnake Springs.
	First major renovation and improvement of cavern lighting begins.
1939	February 10, President Franklin Roosevelt signed legislation adding approximately 39,000 acres to the park, including Slaughter Canyon.
	June 2, Robert Ripley (*Ripley's Believe It or Not*) makes radio broadcast from Rock of Ages hill.
1940	May 10, Sewage system and first flush toilets go into service in the underground lunchroom area.
1943	April, Shortcut under Iceberg Rock is constructed.
1944	May, Superintendent's office moves from town of Carlsbad into park.
1945	September 8, Visitor fee for elevator use is eliminated.
1946	April 26, Jim White dies.
1948	January, First Park Ranger is permanently stationed at Rattlesnake Springs.
	September, Sloth bones are found at Devil's Den.
1949	June 8, Commercial electric power begins at park, replacing the park generator.
1951	Paving of Cavern trail begins.
1952	August 19, Tex Helm takes the "Big Shot" photo of the Big Room using 2400 flashbulbs.
1953	Paving of existing trails is completed.
1954	January, Bat Cave seating area completed.
	March, Iceberg Rock seating area is completed.
1955	New elevators installed and put into service. First fluorescent lights are installed in Cavern.
	May, Top of the Cross seating area is completed.
1957	May, Carlsbad Caverns Natural History Association is incorporated. (Current name: Carlsbad Caverns - Guadalupe Mountains Association)
	March, Stairway from Iceberg Rock to Green Lake Room is replaced by incline trail.
1957	August, Camel bones are found in Slaughter Canyon Cave (New Cave).
	September, All guano mining operations halted at Slaughter Canyon Cave (New Cave); by the end of September, all mining equipment is removed from cave.
1958	January, Jaguar bones are found at Slaughter Canyon Cave.
	January 20, A quit claim deed from Myrtle G. Blakely is recorded at the Eddy County Courthouse in Carlsbad for 40 acres of land, which included Bat Cave.

About the same time, Texan Abijah Long found the Cavern's second, smaller entrance while grazing his mules one day. Descending by rope, he found himself among the bats, their guano almost up to the 90-foot ceiling in places. The business potential for fertilizer overwhelmed his mind, and he filed a mining claim on March 28, 1903.

White became Long's foreman, in large part to explore the cave when he could. At first, the miners built a rail system with ore cars to haul the guano out the Natural Entrance. Later they sank shafts directly into Bat Cave, erected a hoist tower on the surface, and put a guano bucket and pulley system into operation. They transported the guano to town over a primitive wagon road they cleared down the 45-percent-grade hill.

Photo credit—NPS

Colonel Tom Boles (in car) and Jim White (seated on running board) were two of the pioneers whose hard work was important in bringing the cave's wonders to public view. White built a guano bucket "elevator" system to take the first visitors into the cave.

The biggest market for the guano was Southern California, where orange groves were being planted. Low prices, high costs, and processing problems kept Long from making money, however, and he sold his claim. Six other companies would try their hand at Carlsbad's guano industry over the next two decades, but none would really succeed.

White remained with the mining operations through the changes, exploring more than half the known Cavern and naming many formations and rooms. He wanted everyone to see his "Bat Cave," but interested visitors were few. Climbing the road, an early visitor wrote, was like driving up a flight of stairs. One needed to take an extra axle and tires for repairs along the way. Then there was the "elevator." Visitors were lowered 170 feet into Bat Cave by the guano bucket and hoist. It took a nerve-wracking hour to lower 20 people. The "trail" was simply the best route through boulders and around ledges, and White claimed sometimes he had to blindfold visitors to get them through a section.

One day in 1915 White said he decided to do everything he could to bring the world to see "his" cave. He started moving rocks and leveling paths to make a better trail, at steep places driving auto axles from the junkyard into the rocks and stringing wire handholds between them. Then he asked local photographer Ray V. Davis to come see the cave, hoping Davis would take photos to prove its magnificence to the skeptics.

Davis was enchanted from his first look at the King's Palace, and he began working in the cave regularly. Over the next few years, he'd pioneer cave photography and play a significant role in bringing the Cavern to the world's attention. He made a hundred trips into the cave — carrying 75-100 pounds of equipment from the entrance by himself. At first Davis took only close-ups, but as he learned to control the lighting, he shot wider scenes with flashes in separate locations. His multiple-flash technique, using magnesium powder, produced depth that had never been attained before. His method was not only dangerous but produced a great deal of white smoke, which had to clear before Davis could shoot again. Sometimes he could make only one picture a day, at a cost of $15.

Even with Davis' pictures as evidence, people didn't believe the Cavern's wonder. So in September 1922, Davis set up a tour for prominent Carlsbad citizens. Forty signed up; 13 showed up. One of them was S.L. Perry, editor of the Carlsbad *Current-Argus*. Perry wrote up the tour for his paper: "Words are inadequate to convey it to the mind. You can never appreciate its beauty and grandeur unless you see it...." With this publicity, the tide turned and visitors started coming almost daily.

By spring of 1923, Davis was exhibiting his Cavern photos in his studio and putting them in hotels throughout the Southwest. White was advertising his guide service in the *Current-Argus*: "Bat Cave Guide. Sightseers wishing a guide for exploring the California Bat Caves will find me at the cave, or Weaver's garage while in Carlsbad. I charge $2.00 per person per day, when not less than 5 in a party...."

On May 5, another skeptic showed up. Robert Holley from the General Land Office had been instructed to survey the Cavern and report on the possibility of securing it as a national monument. Holley expected this to be a little job taking but a few hours, but it took over a month, during which time Holley became duly impressed. The report he wrote began, "I enter upon this task with a feeling of temerity as I am wholly conscious of the feebleness of my efforts to convey in words the deep conflicting emotions, the feelings of fear and awe, and the desire for an inspired understanding of the Divine Creator's work which presents to the human eye such a complex aggregate of natural wonders in such a limited space." He recommended national monument designation for the Cavern.

The program for the Carlsbad July 4th festivities that year announced on its cover, "Visit the Carlsbad Mammoth Cave." Cars left from town hotels at 7 a.m. with sightseers. One of the visitors that summer was El Paso attorney Richard Burgess. After his visit, he wrote to the U.S. Geological Survey for a map of the Cavern, and geologist Willis T. Lee got the correspondence. Lee was a noted member of the scientific establishment, with high political connections.
He also knew how to work up publicity.

1959	March, Construction of the current visitor center is complete; old stone buildings near cave entrance is removed and tour operations are transferred to the visitor center. Adjacent parking areas, originally constructed in 1940 as overflow, now used as primary parking, with the lower parking area designated as overflow and bat flight parking.
1963	Bat flight amphitheater at the Natural Entrance is constructed and placed into operation, first requested some 16 -17 years earlier as seating area for bat flight viewers.
1966	June 26, Guadalupe Room is discovered.
1967	June, Self-guided trips through the Big Room are begun. Rangers stationed at points throughout the Big Room interpret their section as visitors pass by.
1972	January 6, Self-guided tours of entire Cavern are initiated.
1975 to 1977	Cavern's lighting system is replaced.
1977	January, Current lighting and wiring system completed. Emergency light system is installed, eliminating use of lanterns during power failures.
1978	November 10, Under Public Law 95-625, 33,125 acres of Carlsbad Caverns National Park is designated as wilderness.
1981	Ten other caves in the park open for recreational caving with permits issued subject to skills and experience of applicants.
1984	June, A group of Colorado cavers receives permission to dig in the already disturbed floor of Lechuguilla Cave (only 200' long) to investigate "blowing leads." May 31, 1986, Lechuguilla Cave is surveyed at 3500' long and 703' deep.
1988	The Caverns Historic District and the Rattlesnake Springs Historic District are created. May 30, Lechuguilla Cave now stretches 16 miles in length and measures 1501' deep.
1994	April, Lechuguilla Cave surpasses 70 miles in known passage way.
1995	December, Carlsbad Caverns National Park becomes a World Heritage Site.
1998	Park celebrates 75th anniversary of proclamation as a National Monument.

Lee was already scheduled to go check out an irrigation reservoir site near Carlsbad, so he added the Cavern to his itinerary. Upon touring it, he was impressed, writing, "Had I been told before entering it that an open space of such great dimension was to be found underground, I frankly should have doubted my informants words as frankly as my readers will doubt mine."

The National Geographic Society, having gotten wind of Lee's visit, called him for a story. Lee already had it in hand. It described the Cavern as "the most spectacular of underground wonders..." and was scheduled for the January 1924 *National Geographic*. Now that Lee had the Society's interest, he wanted an expedition. He knew the Society was interested in archaeology, so he wrote to one of Carlsbad's amateur archaeologists, Carl Livingston, telling him to "Procure for me the skull of an ancient man." Livingston, by chance, had a friend who had one decorating his piano. Livingston sent it to Lee, who took it to the National Geographic Society. The results were immediate: the Society provided $16,000 to Lee for the "National Geographic Expedition."

Meanwhile, on October 25, 1923, President Calvin Coolidge had signed a proclamation creating Carlsbad Cave National Monument, 719.22 acres to be administered under the National Park Service (NPS). Lee's expedition arrived the following March. Each morning, Lee wrote, they found themselves "dangling at the end of a line" as they descended by guano bucket. The record thrill ride was taken by *National Geographic* photographer Jacob Gayer, who barely made it out of the bucket when the hoistman prematurely pulled it up, then barely made it out from under the bucket before the hoistman sent it speeding down again.

The expedition found Indian artifacts in the entrance and explored Lower Cave via a twisting ladder that White installed near the Jumping Off Place. The expedition was a grand success, reported on in the September 1925 *National Geographic*. This story introduced the Cavern to the cultured across America, but millions still knew nothing about it.

By the mid 1920s, two thousand people a year were visiting the Cavern, and the first major improvements began. The Carlsbad Chamber of Commerce funded construction of a stairway down the Natural Entrance — 216 wooden steps zig zagging down the slope. A new road up Walnut Canyon, a parking lot, a ticket office, and a chief guide's house were built. Telephones were installed in the cave, and the three-mile tour route was gradually lighted with primitive, generator-powered electric lighting.

In the midst of this development, in May 1927, Colonel Tom Boles became the monument's first superintendent. He brought exactly the mix of talents the Cavern needed at the time and would enthusiastically lead important Cavern development over the next 19 years. Boles focused on bringing more people to the cave and providing the facilities they needed to have a quality experience. He gave talks to visitors, hosted weddings in the Cavern, and created a network of informers to notify him when celebrities were coming. He would make them Cavern boosters and send them out to tell their fans. His efforts paid off. Hollywood directors filmed a newsreel of the bats, as well as scenes for the movies *Haunted Underworld* and *The Medicine Man*. In the 1930s the Santa Fe railroad pho-

It took a nerve-wracking hour to lower a tour of 20 visitors by guano bucket from the surface into Bat Cave 170 feet below.

Photo credit—NPS

tographed its ads in the Cavern, with models clad in evening dresses standing at the foot of giant stalagmites.

By 1930, the Cavern was hosting one hundred thousand visitors per year, and there were an estimated 23 miles of explored passages. There had been a bill introduced to make the Cavern a national park, but politics threatened it. Again, the Cavern needed publicity. Onto the scene strode Frank Ernest Nicholson, journalist and self-proclaimed explorer. Nicholson had a magnetic — some said arrogant — personality with a writing style to match. He convinced the *New York Times* to finance him to explore the "uncharted depths" of the cave and carry his stories to 20 million Americans.

Nicholson's overblown goals were to find another entrance to the Cavern (and build an underground hotel there), find the "lost river" that had created the Cavern (on which visitors would travel to the hotel), find the bats' hibernating place, gather specimens from the cavern (illegal), including "giant amphibians" (nonexistent), and examine the ceiling of the Big Room from a hot air balloon. The expedition was well-equipped, with rubber boats, hip boots "for the swamps," the Goodyear racing balloon, and Nicholson's police dog, Jerry, "for protection in the cave."

From the beginning, the offbeat expedition went awry. The radioman was caught without a license and one of the party was apprehended for stealing stalactites. Still, Nicholson daily wrote about his descent into "Stygian darkness...toward the miles of unknown inferno," describing such adventures as getting lost for eight days (really two hours), during which the bats supposedly fed him. Of his lost river, he wrote, "Obviously it was once of titanic proportions, but now dry, with sand dunes...rising from ten to fifteen feet in height." In reality, it was a dried-up stream, once two inches deep.

The *Times* finally cut off Nicholson's funds, but his stories had already brought the Cavern to millions of people. This publicity likely helped push Congress to pass the park bill, and on May 14, 1930 President Hoover signed into law the establishment of Carlsbad Caverns National Park.

Archaeological and paleontological work began in the new national park. Eventually, the park would be shown to have over

Photo credit—William R. Halliday Collection

By the 1930s the Cavern had become a favorite subject of the media. The Santa Fe railroad photographed an entire ad campaign in the cave. Here, models clad in evening dresses pose in the Hall of Giants in the Big Room.

Photo credit—William R. Halliday Collection

Since the early days, exploration of the Cavern has continued, adding new rooms and miles of passages to the inventory. Lake of the Clouds was discovered in 1930 and marks the deepest known point in the Cavern, 1,037 feet beneath the surface.

The first feastgiver stood at the edge of the steaming mescal pit, her mescal in her hands. In spite of the heat, she was dressed to honor the occasion, in a long cotton dress and high doeskin moccasins. Joey and Nathaniel made blessings, and Evelyn, the tribe's guiding elder, said prayers in Apache. The feastgiver threw her mescal into the pit, and the 30 others we'd harvested were thrown after it. Then several men covered them with damp grama grass, burlap, and dirt until the pit became a mound. Now, the succulent mescal would bake and steam for three days, while we all celebrated.

one hundred sites from as far back as the Pleistocene. In 1930 the University of Pennsylvania Museum directed a dig near the park, finding evidence of both Paleo and Archaic Period Indians. With it they found bones of extinct Pleistocene species, such as bison, musk ox, and antelope, plus the California condor.

In the Cavern, the stairs were replaced by a sloping trail down the Natural Entrance, and the first elevators were built. Sinking the shaft was a major engineering feat — workers started at the top and bottom simultaneously, blasting through solid rock. Amazingly, when they met, they were within one-quarter inch of perfect alignment. Two single-lift elevators — the longest ones in the world — were installed, the project being completed in 1931. Two years later, the park was enlarged from 719 acres to 10,000 acres, and in 1939, President Franklin Roosevelt signed legislation adding 39,000 acres.

From 1938 to 1942 Civilian Conservation Corps workers lived at Rattlesnake Springs while working on construction projects in the park. They built houses, retaining walls, and drainage ditches and other projects. On one occasion the "CC Boys" carried four two-ton electrical cables into the cave.

World War II came and went, taking with it an era of Cavern history, for in 1946 Jim White died in Carlsbad, and Boles left to manage a park in his home state of Arkansas. A Cavern improvement project brought commercial lighting, better trail surfaces, and removal of the stairs. Two more elevators were installed; now the 753-foot trip took only 57 seconds. Hollywood showed up again, in 1950 filming scenes for *Night Without Stars* in the Cavern and for *King Solomon's Mines* in the park's New Cave. The year 1955 brought the first live underground TV broadcast and 1959 *Journey to the Center of the Earth*.

In the 1950s surveys of paleontological resources began, which would eventually show the park as having a rich assemblage of Pleistocene fauna. Investigations in the Cavern turned up bones of jaguar, ground sloth, and big brown bats. Other caves yielded a 23,000-year-old camel, a horse ancestor, and a dire wolf.

In 1963 Rattlesnake Springs, the park's water source since the 1930s, was added to the park, giving Carlsbad Caverns National Park a total of 46,766 acres. In 1978 over 33,000 acres of the park were designated as wilderness. By this time, visitation in all national parks had climbed and environmental impacts were taking a toll. In response, NPS managers began to look at the negative effects of past development and to work toward restoring natural conditions. For example, a study of the Mexican free-tailed bats showed the guano mining shafts to be affecting their numbers. The shafts were plugged, and bats have returned to their original roost. Today the emphasis continues on protecting and restoring park resources. This is the legacy of Carlsbad Caverns National Park, for all people and hopefully for all time.

The Cavern's Natural Entrance is the "great hole" that captured Jim White's imagination and led to his discoveries. Today, millions of people from all over the world walk into it each year on their way to explore the Cavern for themselves.

Photo credit—Laurence Parent

At least three hundred people had come to celebrate this important day. We sat on bleachers around the mescal pit as Joey blessed its opening and Nathaniel explained again that the mescal promoted unity — everyone there would get a special blessing from eating it today. Men began to shovel off the dirt. I watched until the first steaming mescal heads were brought out and then left for the powwow area where they would be served.

The first taste of it surprised me — a cross between a yam, a peach, and a nectarine. Later as I munched a second piece, I stood off by myself, watching Evelyn bless babies and serve mescal to everyone. I was thinking about unity, about healing the damage of the past, on the land and between people, when Evelyn suddenly looked up and caught my eye. We smiled at each other the smile of friends. I'm not certain, even now, what else her look spoke to me, but it was something that is deep and wide and starts a new circle of discovery for us all.

On December 6, 1995, Carlsbad Caverns National Park was voted a World Heritage Site by the World Heritage Convention, a United Nations group begun in 1972 to preserve sites of such universal importance that they are considered part of the heritage of all humanity. Since its inception, the program has helped preserve hundreds of sites around the world, including the Great Pyramids of Egypt, Serengeti National Park of Tanzania, Komodo National Park of Indonesia, and numerous sites in the U.S., including the Statue of Liberty and Yellowstone National Park.

The Land chapter three

As I made my way up the trail to Slaughter Canyon Cave, the crystal notes of a flute filled the canyon. Far below, on the canyon floor, a hiker was winding his way up a faint trail, playing a silver flute as he walked. For a moment, I envied this desert Pan, for he had been out in the desert, and I had not yet, having just arrived at the park the night before. The land around me still just looked like a gray-green blur of nothingness. I knew it wasn't. The cold desert — the Northern tundra — had long ago taught me the paradox of arid lands: they look barren, but they're filled with riches.

A rainbow over Hunter's Peak in Guadalupe Mountains National Park, which adjoins Carlsbad Caverns National Park, is a dramatic reminder of the beauty and abundance this arid land holds.

Photo credit—Laurence Parent

The park's desert ecosystem lies within the Guadalupe Mountains, a southern flank of the Rocky Mountains. This is one of the world's great cave areas, with more than 80 known caves in the park. The importance of the geology here brings scientists from all over the world. Surprisingly at first glance, so does the land's biological richness.

Contrary to popular conception, arid lands contain a great diversity of species, and two special factors multiply the parkland's abundance even further. First, it contains a wide range of habitats, from desert lowlands to montane woodlands. Second, it's an ecotone, a "biological crossroads" where different areas meet and mix, resulting in more species. For example, here grow the madrone tree of the south, ponderosa pine of the north, and Chinquapin oak of the east. Of the park's nearly 800 plant, 331 bird, 64 mammal, and 44 reptile and amphibian species, six are federally endangered and eight are state endangered. This is a precious haven for life.

The land, which ranges from 3,595-6,520 feet above sea level, is composed of three elements: the ancient seabed, the reef, and the riparian area of Rattlesnake Springs. Each provides a different habitat for a different community of plants and animals. The ancient seabed is Chihuahuan Desert and desert grassland, or shortgrass prairie. More rain than other deserts and cool winters give the Chihuahuan Desert a completely unique character. When you're on the reef, you're in mountain habitats, where vegetation changes with elevation. The reef is deeply carved by canyons, leaving relatively flat summits. Around the visitor center, these summits are savanna-like plains, where junipers are scattered over large grassy areas. Higher up, junipers give way to oaks, and in the park's highest reaches are woodlands of piñon pine. Rattlesnake Springs, on the seabed, is composed of a spring and its stream.

Arid lands are defined by low, unpredictable rainfall and high temperatures. All their species must find ways to cope with these conditions — and they have. For example, more than in any other environment, life is below ground. Seventy-two percent of animal species in a desert seek shelter underground, in contrast to six percent in a temperate forest. Most are active only at night during summer, and those that move by day stay in the shade. The paradox of an arid land is that a little water, plus a lot of ingenuity, adds up to abundance.

One desert lowland plant with a highly successful strategy is the creosote bush. Its roots reach down 30 feet or more to permanent moisture. Ocotillo has adapted differently. Its long, thorny stems appear greenish-brown and lifeless until it rains. Then suddenly, tiny, deep green leaves cover the length of the stem, and brilliant red flowers appear in clusters. Blooms even appear on plants without leaves. The ocotillo's secret is its green stem, which can photosynthesize and produce enough food to bloom without leaves. When it rains, leaves become a bonus, allowing the plant to build up food reserves.

Succulents — the cacti, yuccas, and agaves — have been modified to conserve and store water. In cacti, leaves have been reduced to thorns, and enlarged green stems both hold water and photosynthesize. Many also have ribs, which allow the plant to expand to absorb water when it rains. Yuccas and agaves store food and water in thick, fleshy leaves. An agave grows as a rosette of leaves close to the ground. After 10-15 years, it has stored enough food to flower, after which it dies. A common park species, the lechuguilla agave, is one of the indicator plants of Chihuahuan Desert. Lechuguilla is a relative of the larger century plant.

These plants provide a wealth of resources. Cactus fruits and pads are eaten by both people and wildlife. Roadrunners nest in prickly pear and cactus wrens amidst the spines of the cholla. The agave's juicy heart once provided the Mescalero people with their primary food, and the flowers, overflowing with nectar, give the hummingbirds theirs. Old-timers called the yucca pod the desert bighorn's candy, because it fattened them in the fall faster than any other food. Indians braided yucca fibers into rope.

The shortgrass prairie grasses of the desert are exquisitely adapted to live with drought. Two-thirds of the grass plant lies underground, in a shallow but wide-spreading root system. This allows it to absorb water quickly and grow fast. Above ground, the long, narrow leaves are arranged so every blade gets sun, maximizing the photosynthesizing surface. The leaves, unlike those of other plants,

Chihuahuan Desert Plants

Desert plants survive dry conditions by storing water in their leaves and stems. Rain is an added bounty that prompts the land to rejoice by bursting into blossom.

Torrey Yucca   Photo credit—Kelly Thomas

Ocotillo   Photo credit—Kelly Thomas

Lechuguilla   Photo credit—Kelly Thomas

grow continually from the base of the stem, so grazing doesn't stop the plant's growth. These grasses are designed to hold their ground against invading shrubs. Perennial bunch-grasses, for instance, grow side branches, or tillers, that form new clumps of grass, which then spread in tussocks over an area, anchoring soil and keeping succulents and shrubs out. Two native grasses, the gramas and the muhlies, are particularly nutritious for wildlife. The gramas, only five to six inches tall, have heads that look like eyelashes.

Photo credit—Laurence Parent

On the drive up Walnut Canyon to the visitors' center, one rises from the old sea bed on the desert floor through the layers of the reef, the vegetation changing with the elevation. Clumps of brilliant-flowered claret cup cactus grow on the reef's rocky slopes.

Arid-land flowers cope with drought and grazing much like grasses. They stay low, except for flowering stems, to minimize water loss, and they keep buds low on their stems to avoid having them grazed off. The park's flowers include bladderwort, sunflower goldeneye, Indian paintbrush, and verbena, which the Mescalero used as a sedative.

Shrubs and trees complete the census of the park's plant life. In the fall, desert sumac turns brilliant scarlet, and its berries ripen to reddish-orange. Indians used to make a lemonade-like drink from them, and 32 species of birds, as well as small mammals, eat them. Apache plume, which grows in clumps along the arroyos, has fluffy clusters of fruits with feathery, purple-tinged tails that inspired the plant's name. The desert willow, a favorite nesting tree for birds, also grows along the arroyos.

One of the park's most common trees is the juniper. These short, scrubby-looking trees are scattered across the flat-topped ridges and in the canyon bottoms. Juniper is well-adapted to the natural fire cycle of arid lands. It can burn to the ground and still re-sprout from its roots. At higher elevations, the piñon pine joins the junipers. It grows slowly, as many arid-land plants do. A trunk 10 inches in diameter may represent 150 years of growth. Among the park's seven species of oak, the most common is gray oak, recognized by its dusty gray-blue leaves. Gambel oak, with its distinctive grayish bark, was a favorite with Indians because it has the least bitter, most edible acorns.

This varied plant life provides a good foundation for the park's many creatures. Insects may not seem important, but they break down the remains of plants and animals and recycle

Photo credit—Monty Smith

them back into the system, replenishing the soil with nutrients. Researchers say the park is one of the richest areas in the state for insect life. There are more than two hundred species of moths, which are the major food of the park's bats, and 10-20 species of grasshoppers, including a newly discovered species.

The park's mule deer feed peacefully in the morning at Rattlesnake Springs and in Walnut Canyon. They prefer to browse on shrubs such as desert willow but are well adapted for aridity with a flexible diet. They can eat seven hundred kinds of plants!

Rodents aerate the soils by digging and provide the main course for many predators. There are 26 species of rodents in the park. The white-ankled mouse builds its nest among rocks and scurries about during the day in search of seeds. Pocket mice dig underground burrows in which they wait out the heat of day. Two species you may see scurrying across roads of the seabed at night are the silky pocket mouse and the kangaroo rat, which bounds along on its hind legs like a kangaroo. Among the larger rodents, you may see the Texas antelope squirrel scampering merrily over cactus spines or the rock squirrel sitting on rocks around the Cavern entrance.

There are three large native hoofed mammals in the park. Mule deer can be seen feeding in the morning at Rattlesnake Springs and along the Walnut Canyon Desert Drive. They're browsers, preferring shrubs, such as catclaw acacia and desert willow, but are adapted for aridity with a flexible diet; they can eat seven hundred kinds of plants, including cactus. Higher in the park, in the pine woodlands of Putman, Yucca, and Rattlesnake canyons is a small population of elk. Finally, there is the pig-like collared peccary, returned from low numbers in the park just in the last decade. A desert mammal, it travels in bands of about 20 and spends its time digging with its snout for food such as agaves, roots, and bulbs.

A diversity of predators keep the herbivores in balance with their food supplies. In spite of the valuable role of predators, attitudes toward them historically have not been positive. Only after Aldo Leopold, founder of modern wildlife management science, had spent the first decades of his career exterminating Mexican wolves from the Southwest, did he himself come to understand their importance. "Conservation is a state of harmony with a friend," he wrote. "You cannot cherish his right hand and chop off his left."

The park's predators include many insects. The darkling beetles, some as big as your thumb, walk around on the hottest days searching for prey, which amazes biologists, because their black bodies absorb the heat. Reptiles reach their peak diversity in arid lands. Several species of lizards can be found among the rocks of the arroyos and canyons, and there are 24 species of snakes in the park, most of them nocturnal. The red racer is one you may see during the day. It moves very quickly, slithering through the underbrush of the foothills.

The mammal predators include the striped and hog-nosed skunks, which can often be seen at night along Walnut Canyon Road. Badgers are occasionally seen at canyon entrances, and the long-tailed weasel is occasionally observed at Rattlesnake Springs. Raccoons are commonly seen at night, as is their relative, the smaller ringtail, which lives in rocky areas. The black bear, once widespread throughout the Guadalupes, is now rare. A lucky visitor in 1992 watched a mother and cub cross the Walnut Canyon Desert Drive road in front of his car.

Photo credit—Brent Wauer

Spring in the desert means cactus blossoms. Birds use the park's cacti for nests, and mule deer use them for food and water. People also have traditionally eaten the fruit, especially the prickly pear's tasty "tunas."

Top: claret cup cactus; left: rainbow cactus; bottom: prickly pear blossoms and saw-toothed leaves of lechuguilla

Photo credit—Tom Algire

Photo credit—Tom Algire

The condition of top predators in an ecosystem tells a great deal about that system's health. The park boasts a diversity of top predators, with mostly stable populations. They include the bobcat and mountain lion, kit fox, gray fox, and coyote. Top predators may sometimes be seen at night along the Walnut Canyon Road to the park or the Walnut Canyon Desert Drive.

Bats and birds are the predators on flying insects. The park hosts 16 bat species. The Mexican free-tailed bat has a large maternity colony in the Cavern. From May-October, almost

Photo credit—Greg W. Lasley

The cave swallow is a special summer resident of the park, visible on the nest at the Cavern entrance and hunting insects in nearby canyons and at Rattlesnake Springs. The park boasts the largest and northernmost colony of this species and the longest-running banding study in the U.S.

a half-million of these bats put on a spectacular show nightly as they fly out to hunt. They can also be seen, along with other bats, at Rattlesnake Springs when they come in to drink from the pond. An easy one to identify is the tiny western pipistrelle, because it flies before sundown. Rattlesnake Springs is also a hotspot for migratory songbirds that breed in North America and spend winters in points south. The area attracts 19 species of flycatchers, including the vermilion flycatcher, the ash-throated flycatcher, and the western kingbird. Thirty-five of the continent's 40 warblers may be found here, as well as many showy birds, such as tanagers and orioles.

The cave swallow is a special summer resident. The park boasts the largest and northernmost colony of this species — about 2,500 birds, visible on their nests at the Cavern and hunting in nearby canyons and at Rattlesnake Springs. The winter range of cave swallows is unknown. In hopes of discovering it, one park researcher has conducted a banding study of the Cavern colony since 1980, making it the longest-running cave swallow study in the U.S.

While this land is extremely rich, prior to the tumultuous changes brought by European settlement, it was even more so. Gone from the parkland today is the beauty and health once given to it by creatures such as the Montezuma quail, black-tailed prairie dog, plains bison, desert bighorn sheep, Pecos gambusia fish, grizzly bear, and Mexican gray wolf. With restoration of parks to pre-European settlement conditions a part of the NPS mission, today the park is working with other government agencies and private groups to restore its ecosystem and some of its extirpated species.

One critical project is grasslands restoration. Before European settlement, the Carlsbad basin was a land of year-round streams and lush shortgrass prairie. Early settlers said there was so much grass it was "a cowman's paradise." Rodents helped keep this prairie in good health by digging. Small bands of bison, pronghorn antelope, and desert bighorn helped by grazing. Lightning helped by igniting fires that cleared out shrubs, thatched out grasses, and created ash, which then recycled nutrients and re-invigorated plant growth.

It was a system perfectly adapted for aridity, but in a delicate balance because it lay at the edge of the desert. Small clumps of desert plants already mixed with grasses. When settlers poured an overwhelming number of cattle, sheep, and goats onto the land, the result was ecological disaster. Under the relentless overgrazing, aided by severe droughts, the native bunchgrasses gave way to desert scrub. The soils, left exposed, were blown away by hot winds and trampled by cattle. The compacted ground could not hold the rain. Instead, the water ran off the land, carving arroyos and swelling streams, ripping away their protective vegetation, silting the water, suffocating the fish, and carrying away more soil, with the nutrients that could re-establish the grassland.

The park's land suffered less than the surrounding basin, but soil and grasses have still been lost. To begin a remedy, livestock grazing was removed in the 1950s, but managers say the prairie's natural rebuilder, fire, must be reintroduced. Speaking of former NPS policies that suppressed natural fire cycles, one manager says, "Fire is a species unto itself that needs to be allowed a space to live in. We have to make fire something other than a captive animal. It has to be free-roaming."

Reaffirming a fire management policy in harmony with the area's natural 12-15 year fire cycle, managers now follow a fire management plan. The plan uses fire as a tool to decrease shrubs and succulents and increase the nutritious native grasses. Following the plan, managers began a series of controlled burns to see what the effects of fire really are. They have found that burned areas have more grasses and fewer succulents and shrubs. Park managers are working with the managers of surrounding public lands to extend the fire plan throughout the Guadalupe Mountains, making it an ecosystem-wide effort.

With a healthier grassland, managers hope to reintroduce species such as Montezuma quail and desert bighorn sheep. The bighorn is now being restored in the state, and long-range plans include reintroducing it in the Guadalupes. It's an "umbrella" species, like the wolf or mountain lion — by virtue of its large home range, restoring it puts an umbrella over all the other species that share its home. Focusing on umbrella species is part of ecosystem management, to which our nation is committed.

The other critical project is restoring Rattlesnake Springs. Riparian areas are the lifeblood of arid lands, and in New Mexico, 90 percent are gone. Rattlesnake Springs is home to several rare and threatened species. Nearly three hundred bird species use this riparian area. Many are the migratory songbirds, which are declining due to habitat loss on both their nesting and wintering grounds. Rattlesnake Springs provides critical nesting sites for the orchard oriole and Bell's vireo.

The nests of songbirds are being parasitized by cowbirds, which once followed the buffalo herds and have increased as a result of livestock grazing. A cowbird adds its egg to the nest of a songbird, which then incubates, hatches, and feeds the cowbird chick

The park boasts a wide range of predators, a fact that signifies the ecosystem's health. Top predators include the mountain lion, kit fox, and coyote. The Mexican gray wolf, now gone from the scene, also once roamed the region.

Photo credit—Alan & Sandy Carey

along with its own. But because the cowbird hatches earlier and grows faster than the songbird's chicks, the latter often don't survive. Bell's vireos lose over 50 percent of their young this way.

The long-term solution, managers feel, lies in restoring the natural riparian area, which the park hopes to do in partnership with its neighbors managing surrounding lands. The first task will be to discover how big the original system was and how it functioned. Historically, the water from the springs created a permanent stream that flowed toward the Black and Pecos Rivers. Road construction blocked the stream flow and shortened the riparian corridor. Scientists used remnant wetland soils underlying the area to map the extent of the original wetland system.

Meanwhile, managers use a Geographical Information System (GIS), a leading-edge computer tool that maps an area's natural resources, to identify and begin pilot projects. Their "wish-list" includes adding to populations of threatened species such as the cricket frog, plain-bellied water snake, and common ground dove; reintroducing a top predator fish, the Pecos gambusia; and ensuring that a 1991 release of native roundnose minnows and greenthroat darters is succeeding.

Photo credit—NPS

Reptiles reach their peak diversity in arid lands. The collared lizard is one of the more uncommon of the park's several lizard species you may see sunning on the rocks of the arroyos and canyons or scurrying into the shade when it gets too warm.

Ken and I turned onto the Walnut Canyon Desert Drive road as the sun was coming up. On the first bend, we surprised a mule deer doe and two fawns standing in the road. More deer browsed ahead in the grassy savanna, dotted with the backlit rosettes of agaves, and I wondered if the deer were eating them much during these days of drought. As we dropped into the canyon, I noticed the gentle swirls of the back reef — geology I hadn't had the eye to see when I first arrived in the park. We flushed an early-rising lizard and group of savanna sparrows as we walked to the pond, which was bone dry. I wondered how the animals that depended upon this place were faring. I felt a little like a worried mother. I had walked the land now, and it was no longer gray-green emptiness to me. It had become the home of my friends.

Photo credit—Gerald & Buff Corsi

The desert bighorn historically roamed the parkland but was extirpated from the area, along with bison and pronghorn antelope, when European settlement arrived. There are long-term plans to restore the bighorn to its native home in the Guadalupes.

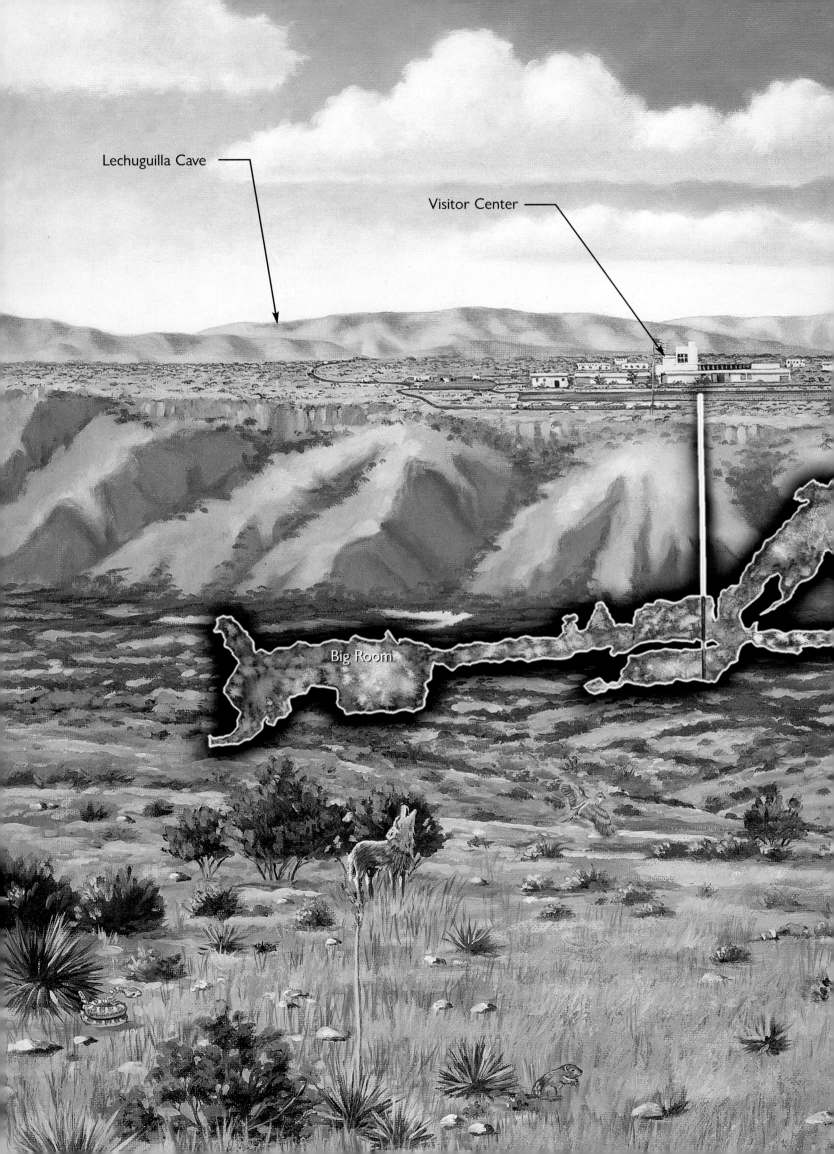

Lechuguilla Cave

Visitor Center

Big Room

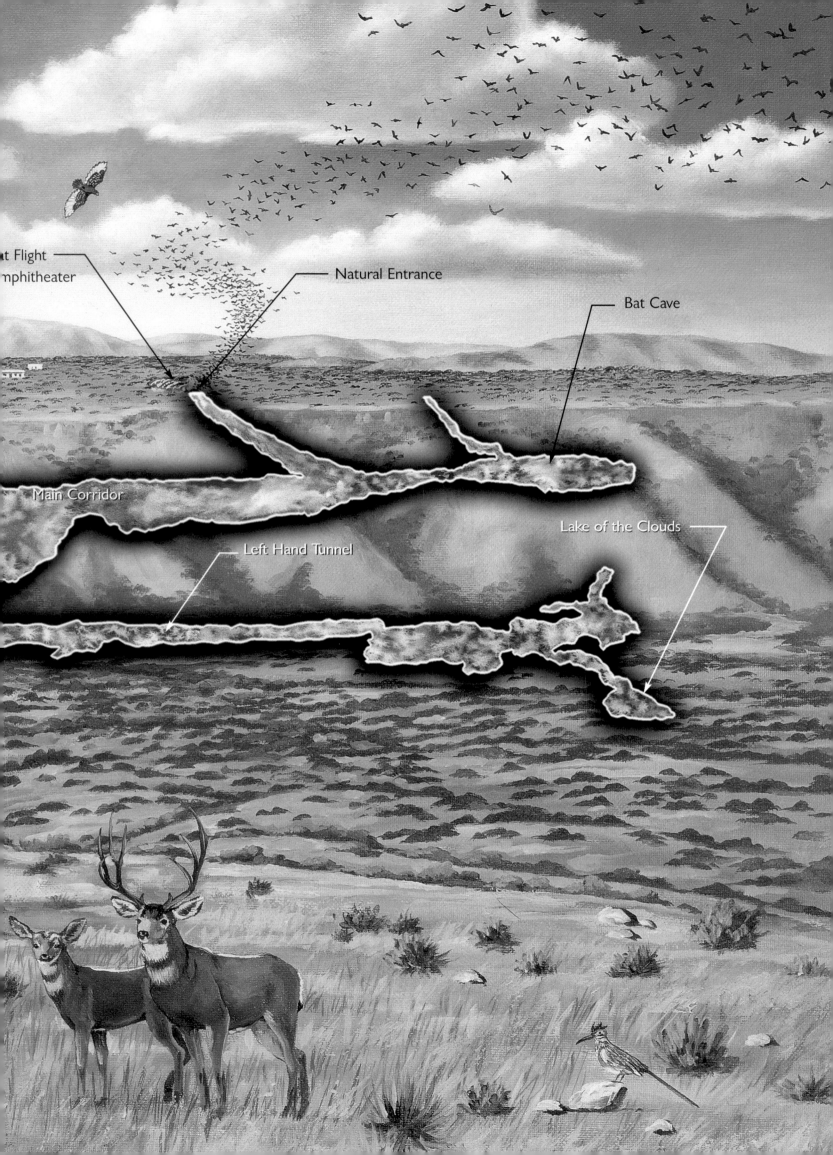

t Flight
mphitheater

Natural Entrance

Bat Cave

Main Corridor

Left Hand Tunnel

Lake of the Clouds

The Cavern

Ken came barrelling — a pace I have absolutely never known him to exhibit — out of the visitor center elevator and headed toward me. He was shaking his head intently, as if something had confused him. I wondered what was wrong. As our eyes met, he broke out laughing, and he kept laughing and shaking his head until he reached me. Finally, he quieted, and his face took on a look of wonder. "It's beyond description," he said.

He was talking about the Big Room, which he had just toured for the first time. Now I was about to go. I gave him a skeptical look and headed for the elevators. The only other commercial cave I'd been in had been a disappointment. The brochure had set me up for gigantic formations and brilliant colors, but the real thing was drab and boring.

As we descended in the elevator, I told myself the Big Room can't be that great. The postcards exaggerate. Ken is just enthralled because he hasn't seen as much of the world as I have. This was going to be a nice cave, but just another cave.

I stepped off the elevator, walked through the revolving doors that act as an airlock, and the Big Room hit me like a pie in the face. Groups of people walked around me as I just stood in the trail, my brain trying to compute the magnificence I was seeing. I thought in all seriousness, "This is the back lot at Disney." And I've been on the back lot at Disney many times. Finally, I was able to squint up at this incredible chandelier that seemed to fill the room with its presence, and I thought, "This is a ballroom for kings."

The Big Room is the largest natural limestone chamber in the U.S., with a length of four thousand feet, a width of 625 feet, and a greatest ceiling height of 255 feet. It covers 57 acres. The centerpiece is the Giant Chandelier, made of ribbon stalactites. Stalactites, which "hang tite" to the ceiling, begin as hollow "soda straws" of calcite. They form as water drips through a fissure. Calcite is deposited around the outside of the drops in a ring. As the soda straw grows, it may become plugged, forcing water back up to the top and then down its outside, building a stalactite. The shape, size, and even texture of a stalactite is determined by the drip rate and other environmental factors. A fast-growing one tends to be long and thin, while a slow-growing one becomes fat and stubby.

Down the trail is the Lion's Tail, a "war club" formation. Its bulbous end is covered with cave popcorn, which forms by condensation. The level to which popcorn grows in the Big Room shows where condensation is occurring. You can see this "popcorn line" on the Lion's Tail itself. Above it, the stone is bare and corroded.

I came to the Hall of Giants, three huge stalagmites. Stalagmites are created when water falls from the ceiling or from a stalactite. Water falling quickly over a long distance splashes over a wide area to result in massive formations like these. Giant Dome is actually a column, which results when a stalactite and stalagmite meet. It's the tallest formation in the Big Room, 60 feet high, with a base circumference of one hundred feet.

Fairyland is an area of popcorn-covered stalagmites 2-1/2 to four feet tall. It's one of my favorite areas in the Cavern, because it touches the child in me. She's convinced that elves created Fairyland and live there now, coming out to play each night. Just beyond Fairyland is a gigantic 25-foot-tall column, Temple of the Sun. The largest columns are typically aligned beneath ceiling fractures, where the greatest amount of water enters a cave.

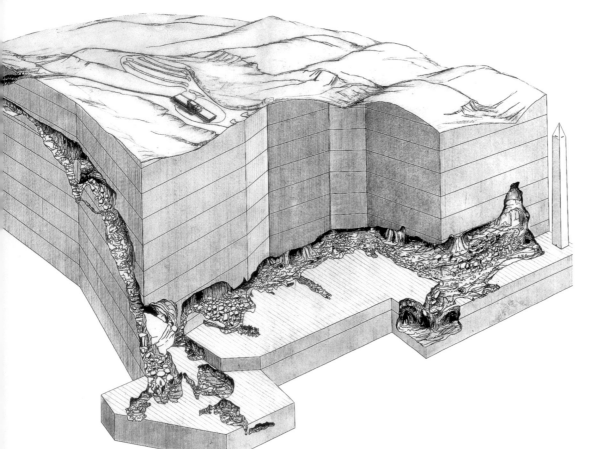

The Giant Chandelier, made of ribbon stalactites, forms an awesome center-piece in the Big Room. Its creation began about 800,000 years ago, as water from the surface dripped into the Cavern and deposited tiny rings of calcite on the ceiling.

This cutaway view of the Cavern shows its orientation to the surface and the three miles of trails descending 830 feet into the mountain.

Page 31

Down the trail is the Jumping Off Place, which overlooks Lower Cave, 93 feet below. Jim White explored it by rope, and later, for Dr. Lee's research expedition, cut rungs from trees in Walnut Canyon and built a ladder of wire and wood. Seventy-five feet of it swung free of the wall, and those who descended did so unhappily. Lee's assistant, Carl Livingston, wrote, "You would get halfway down when the ladder would...begin to spin. Part of the time you would have your face to the wall and part of the time your back would be against it and your feet fighting to find a rung."

Next stop is the Top of the Cross. The Big Room is shaped like a cross, or T. Look up on the ceiling here and you'll see the fractures, or joints, in the rock that created this shape. That ceiling area was first explored in 1985. Cavers used helium balloons to lift and secure a cord to a stalagmite near the ceiling. Then they tied a climbing rope to the cord and pulled it up around the stalagmite. When they climbed up, they discovered eight hundred feet of passage, which they named Spirit World. The cord still marks their entry.

Mirror Lake is a drip pool, like the Cavern's other "lakes" and "springs." They're fed by infiltrating surface water. Scattered over the surface are lily pads, a type of calcite formation Lee described as "a thin sheet of onyx which grew from a center in concentric rings outward to a knife edge....The edge of the lily pads represents the former level of the water in the fountain [pool]. Now that the basin is dry, they stand forth like campstools."

Next is Bottomless Pit, an apt name, since the soft silt bottom keeps objects from making a sound when they hit. Although it's actually only 140 feet deep, mystery has surrounded it since the early days. In 1929 Amelia Earhart visited the Cavern and planned a return trip to descend into the Pit after her flight around the world. Park managers find all sorts of things at the bottom that visitors have thrown in — even a wedding ring.

Around the bend, huge white iceberg-like blocks of gypsum lie scattered to the left of the trail. Usually white, gypsum is one of the three most common minerals in Guadalupe caves, the others being calcite and aragonite. The abundance of gypsum is a clue to the sulfuric origin of the caves, because the byproduct of sulfuric acid dissolving limestone is gypsum. When the Cavern was young, gypsum covered its floors, but so much water entered from the surface that most of it was dissolved and carried away.

Abundant water in the distant past is also the key to the amount of decoration in the Cavern. When the climate began to dry, most formations stopped growing, and today 95 percent of them are dormant. Crystal Springs Dome is the largest one still active — the fractures and pores in the rock in this area allow water to reach the Dome routinely. Because these water pathways vary throughout the cave, so does the time it takes rainwater to reach formations, from two weeks to more than a year.

Crystal Springs Dome shows the Cavern's water cycle at work. Speleothems only grow when surface water reaches them. On average only 13 inches of rain per year falls in the Carlsbad area, and the thirsty earth drinks up much of it before it reaches the Cavern. So most of the time the cave is drying out. But every five to ten years there is a lot of rain, which recharges the cave system. At those times, dormant formations may begin to grow, and places such as Crystal Springs Dome look like a firehose has been turned on them.

The 1928 *Cavern Guide* described the Rock of Ages as "probably the handsomest stalagmite in the whole cave." In addition to good looks, it has more history surrounding it than any Cavern formation. Superintendent Tom Boles instituted the Rock of Ages ceremony here, which ran from 1927-1944. After people were seated, all the lights in the Big Room were turned out. Then, as a ranger quartet sang *Rock of Ages*, the lights were brought up gradually, beginning with those most distant. It was the most famous special lighting show ever known in a cave. For Boles, it was a pet project, and he often hosted special events here. They included Will Rogers' visit in 1931, when Rogers remarked he was "glad they gave God the credit for these underground wonders instead of the Republican Party."

At the Painted Grotto and Doll's Theater, the Cavern's natural color blushes through. Calcite, gypsum, and aragonite are clear or white in their natural states, but minerals such as iron and manganese create tints. Both of these areas have long soda straws tinted a delicate peach from iron oxide. Doll's Theater had more soda straws until a visitor threw an orange into it, breaking many of them.

The following day, I toured the Natural Entrance with one of the rangers. The first thing I discovered is that a cave is not a black hole. It's an intricate group of ecosystems, most of which are characterized by stable temperatures, lightlessness, and little food.

However, the first zone, the entrance, has lots of light, lots of food being brought in from outside, and a diversity of invertebrates that move between the cave and the surface. Researchers studied Cavern invertebrates in the late 1980s and found that the Cavern has an abundance. Bacteria and fungi break down dead material and recycle it back into the system. Springtails and colombola eat the fungi. Predators — mites, pseudoscorpions, spiders, three species of cave crickets, and beetles — eat everything. Seven species of bats bring in a rich source of food from the outside that benefits all.

Photo credit—NPS

Sometimes trace minerals in the water that was decorating the cave brought in colors— reds from manganese and orange tones from iron oxide. The Painted Grotto is one of the few such areas in the Cavern.

Photo credit—NPS/Russ Finley

On the way down the steep Natural Entrance trail, visitors walk past the Devil's Den. Named by Jim White, it's a two-hundred-foot dropoff that White tried repeatedly to find a way around, but couldn't. Most of the Cavern's present trail follows White's original route.

Man has also used the entrance for hundreds of years. A prehistoric midden ring lies outside the entrance. Just inside, high on the wall, are pictographs created by early people, and part of a sandal was found during construction of the Natural Entrance trail.

Photo credit—NPS

A rare shaft of light penetrates the twilight zone of the Cavern's Natural Entrance. The twilight zone of a cave extends as far as there is light enough for a human to see.

Temperatures in the cave vary, depending on air flow from the outside. Especially in winter, the cavern is affected by its large entrance and by its location in an arroyo. As warm cave air rises, it is displaced by cold air sweeping down the arroyo and into the cave. This effect cools major portions of the cave, including the Big Room, to 56 degrees Fahrenheit. Away from these areas the cave warms up to 68 degrees.

Beyond the entrance is the twilight zone, which extends as far as there is enough light for a human to see. A resident of this zone is the cave swallow. Arriving in February to breed, the swallows build little cup nests of mud on the Cavern wall and re-use them year after year. Both parents help raise their young, hunting insects for them near the Cavern in early morning and late afternoon. Frequently some are still out when the bats begin flying. They're highly gregarious birds that constantly interact and chatter at one another, and they're fun to watch.

Beyond the twilight zone is the dark zone. Temperatures are more stable, darkness total, and food so scarce that few species can survive. Those that do survive have adapted to the conditions. Some still go to the surface for food. Others have evolved into cave dwellers. They've lost eyes, color, and other attributes that don't work here and developed others that do. They can't survive outside the cave. Two of the Cavern's cricket species stand at the opposite ends of cave adaptation, and each dominates in a different area accordingly. Adaptations include a slimmer, paler, and longer body, lower metabolism and reproduction, and the ability to subsist on little food. *Ceuthophilus longipes* is the most cave-adapted cricket, found in food-poor areas. *Ceuthophilus carlsbadensis* dominates in food-rich areas.

One of the places *longipes* is found is in Sand Passage. Although it has little food, it's a good place to lay eggs, for the floor is deep carbonate sand. A cave cricket's biggest predator is also here: rhadine beetles, which search endlessly for cricket eggs. Using antennae sensitive to touch as well as chemicals left by the egg-laying crickets, the rhadine probes the sand until it finds an egg, digs it out, punctures the shell, and pumps the contents into its mouth. The egg is almost as big as the beetle and supplies it with food for days. *Longipes* has responded to this predation by evolving the ability to bury eggs deeper.

As we walked, I caught a strong but pleasant musty fragrance. The turnoff for the Mexican free-tailed bat maternity colony was just a quarter mile away. Early explorers described it colorfully. Nicholson wrote, "Ahead of us there appeared to be gigantic curtains of black velvet draped far down from the ceiling. A moment later the festoons of black drapery began to slowly move, and I realized they were thousands of bats clinging to each other....The odor was stifling, the noise stupefying, and yet the grandeur and magnitude of it all held us spellbound." Since the mining shafts were plugged in 1981, the bats have been returning to this area. Park managers have set up photomonitoring points that, over time, will provide accurate population trends.

The bat guano is such a rich food source that it supports the largest invertebrate community in the Cavern. Researchers say there are five to ten thousand invertebrates in a cup of guano during bat season. There are mites in the billions, pseudoscorpions, and the darkling beetles of the desert walking on the mounds of guano. Spiders' webs, draped with guano, hang from the walls. *Carlsbadensis* roams the surface, eating guano and other crickets. Once the bats leave, though, this rich community crashes. The cup of guano now holds one hundred invertebrates, many from just one family of mite.

Jim White wasn't given to fear. But the name he chose for Devil's Spring when he discovered it on his first trip into the Cavern reminded me that he had nothing more than a coffee pot-looking miner's lantern, which threw little more light than a candle. His imagination concerning what lay beyond must have run wild. Across a two-hundred-foot dropoff from this Spring are the Devil's Den, Shade Tree, and Lawn Chair. The Devil's Den stopped White's exploration for some time; he made six trips across it trying to find a better route but couldn't. He once said this was the closest to hell he ever planned to get. The Devil's Lawn Chair is a curved stalagmite; the Shade Tree is popcorn on the wall.

Our trail had so far been winding down — steeply, which the ranger says can be hard on senior citizens — through the layers of limestone that were laid over eons in the ancient sea. Here, at the Whale's Mouth, we entered the massive Capitan Reef itself. Soon, we were at the Devil's Hump. White routinely shepherded people through this extremely dangerous section without anyone ever being injured. Lee described White's excellence as a guide: "We proceeded at a snail-like pace through heaps of fallen rock and over ledges where he patiently showed the bewildered climber which foot to put forward in order that the next step may be taken in safety."

On the other side of Devil's Hump lies Iceberg Rock, a fallen section of the ceiling. Most of the "breakdown," the rocks and rubble you see along the trail, fell long ago when water drained from the passages. The two-hundred-thousand ton Iceberg Rock fell much more recently, still about three hundred thousand years ago. We know the huge rock fell more recently than most because on the underside we see stalactites that formed after the cave was dry.

The Boneyard to the right also represents a stage in Cavern development. Here, the water followed many cracks and fissures and dissolved a three-dimensional maze of passages rather than typical large rooms. A feature that occurs throughout Guadalupe caves, "boneyard" looks harmless but is an easy place to get lost. Some boneyard in Lechuguilla cave is over three hundred feet thick.

Our tour complete, I said so long to the ranger and returned later that day to walk the trail with resource managers and talk about what's going on "behind the scenes." Take the trail, for instance. Much of the route is still Jim White's original; current improvements are focused on better handrails and trail surfaces. Handrails are important, because they deter people from getting off-trail and damaging the cave. Park managers have chosen to use stainless steel because it doesn't corrode in the cave air, but the cost is high — $150,000 for the three-mile trail through the Natural Entrance and Big Room. NPS budgets don't allow expenses of this size, so the rails are being added as there is money available.

The current elevators date from 1998. Revolving doors were added as an airlock in 1976. A microclimatologist had discovered the elevator shaft was contributing to drying the Cavern by pulling moist cave air out. Of the 750,000 Cavern visitors each year, about one quarter of them ride the elevator down and all of them ride it back up to the surface. The elevators make 49,000 round trips per year, traveling close to 14,000 miles.

Today's lighting system uses more than a thousand bulbs and tubes that range from 60-1,500 watts and are controlled by 16 separate circuits using 19 miles of concealed wires. The system's design principles include use of low-intensity light, use of darkness and contrast as design elements, and lighting to reveal the Cavern's natural beauty. Thus, no colored lights are used, only various shades of white.

I asked about management problems. The largest is the breaking and taking of formations. When ranger-guided tours were converted to self-guided ones in the 1970s, this irretrievable loss grew to wholesale proportions. Studies showed over 18,000 formations had been broken over an eight-year period. As a result, the park instituted guided tours in the fragile King's Palace area and installed guide rails to keep visitors on the trails. These measures have had a positive impact on the level of vandalism, although problems still occur.

Other impacts from visitation are less purposeful, and some are simply part of human presence. I learned that people throw so many coins into the pools, for example, they must be cleaned out weekly. Even the low-level lighting casts enough light for algae to grow on formations, and people's clothes leave lint behind. The cave resource manager said, "This cave has really seen a lot of suffering."

Another visitor on the trail approached us and asked us to shine our flashlight on Giant Dome's flutings, which are actually small draperies. They form when water runs down a curved surface, such as an arched ceiling, continually following the same track. A ridge forms that builds into a ribbon, and finally a drapery, sometimes with folds extending to the floor.

Ongoing restoration efforts on the main tour route are handled by NPS staff and volunteer groups, such as Carlsbat Cavers. Started in 1990 by Carlsbad residents who saw a need for cleanup, the group has grown to about 45 local people. They help keep trails, pools, and formations clean and repair broken formations with epoxy. In 1995, the Carlsbat Cavers spent three thousand hours volunteering for such work.

Other volunteers, called VIPs, apply to work at the park in an area of their interest for a specified length of time, from a weekend to a season. VIPs allow the park to complete projects that otherwise sit for lack of staff.

The Cave Research Foundation (CRF) has been doing volunteer exploration since the 1960s and has helped increase the Cavern's discovered passages. CRF also restores areas damaged in the past. For example, people have tracked mud and grit over the flowstone in the New Mexico Room since it was discovered in the 1920s. Because the room is still active, the grit can become cemented into new deposits. CRF members clean the stone so that won't happen and repair eroded trails so there is only one way to walk.

I was looking forward to seeing the elaborate cake-frosting decoration of the King's Palace. Holley had called it a fairyland. But my first King's Palace tour wasn't what I'd expected. Early on, a pleasant grandmotherly woman struck up a conversation, remarking about the beauty of the formations. Her name was Edie. She and her husband were here from New York for their first visit. At first, I wanted her to leave me alone so I could concentrate on the tour. But she was so filled with wonder about the cave — just as Ken had been. I remembered what he'd said at dinner the night before: "Environmental work is like building a speleothem. You do it one drip at a time." Not that Edie was a drip! She was a chance to deposit one.

So with a changed perspective, when she remarked on the beauty of a drapery we were passing, I replied, "Yes, it is beautiful, and look how it's broken off here. The biggest problem this cave has is vandalism." I was unprepared for the strength of Edie's response. She stopped walking, and a concerned expression clouded her face. She looked me in the eye. "That's terrible," she replied, and she meant it.

Encouraged, I went on with the other statistics. When I got to the part about the orange in Dolls Theater, her concern turned to horror. She blurted out, "I'm appalled. I've got grandkids and I want there to be something left for them to see. This is my park, too." We started walking again, but she was on a roll. "You know, I write letters to my Congressmen all the time about things. Nothing's going to change if we don't make it change. I'll write a letter about this. I will. As soon as I get home." Her husband called her and she scurried up the trail toward him, talking to herself about getting this vandalism stopped. I have no doubt she wrote that letter — and that her Congressman listened.

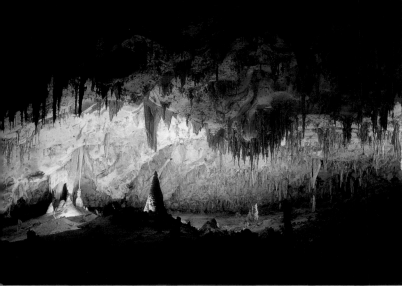

Photo credit—John Dittle

The King's Palace is one of the most ornately decorated portions of the Cavern. Rooms filled with drape upon drape of all lengths, delicate stalactites, and an abundance of fluted column stalagmites make this area worthy of its name.

The Bats

The bat flight amphitheater at the entrance to Carlsbad Cavern is alive with excitement. As the sun sinks, the stands are filling up with chattering, laughing people anticipating what is to come. Even the cave swallows are hinting that something important is about to happen, swooping over the theater and calling loudly.

The ranger begins her program, barely, when a murmur goes up from the crowd. There they are: just a couple of fluttery things, smaller than the swallows, drifting out from the Cavern's entrance. In response to the crowd, the ranger turns toward the entrance and sees the bats. "Well, hello there!" she greets them. That's it. The ranger's bat program is over and the one by the bats has begun.

Now a slim thread of bats emerges, swirling silently upward from the entrance in a living funnel. At the top of the funnel, streamers of bats break off and float toward the river valleys 10-25 miles away to hunt insects for the night. The thread quickly thickens, and thousands pour out by the minute. The sky blackens with them, tiny silhouettes against the deepening sky. As they fly away, they swirl into smoke-like clouds, filling the distant horizon with undulating puffs. The clouds float further and further away until they are out of sight. I am reminded of how smoke is sacred to Native Americans; it is the vehicle on which they send prayers to their Creator. I think how apt it is the bats look like smoke.

As the hour wears on, the sky behind the bat-clouds becomes a wash of cerise and purple. Then it, too, fades, as the full moon rises. And the bats are still flying silently out of the cave.

To many visitors, the nightly emergence of Carlsbad Cavern's famous Mexican free-tailed bats is one of the greatest wildlife spectacles they have ever seen. Mexican freetails are the park's most numerous bat species, but not the only one. Sixteen species of these amazing flying mammals have been identified in the park.

Most scientists believe bats evolved at least 55 million years ago from a small shrew-like animal that glided between trees. Today, there are nearly one thousand species, living everywhere except the Antarctic and high Arctic. About 70 percent eat insects, including many agricultural pests. Most others feed on fruit and flower parts. All the park's species are insectivores.

Bats are mammals, like us. But unlike us, they fill an extremely specialized niche in the animal world. To equip them for this role, they are adapted in amazing ways.

Chiroptera, the Greek name for bats' taxonomic order, means "hand-wing." Bats have arms, hands, and fingers with all the same bones as humans. But in bats the fingers are elongated, and a thin skin membrane stretches between them, forming a wing. A clawed thumb is left free for grasping. Many bats also have a membrane between their hind legs and tails.

Wings are shaped for a bat's lifestyle. Bats that travel distances and hunt insects in open areas have long, narrow wings good for fast, direct flight but poor for lift and maneuvering. Our Mexican free-tailed bats, known as the speedsters of the bat world, have this type of wing. Other bats, including most that feed on fruit or nectar, have short, wide wings, allowing them to hover, maneuver, and carry heavy loads.

Because flying requires a great deal of energy, bats have a heavy-duty cardiovascular system. Their hearts are large in proportion to their size, and their heartbeats range from a normal of two hundred beats per minute to as high as one thousand per minute in flight. Their unique circulatory system makes them valuable for studying human cardiovascular problems.

While they can increase their metabolism for the demands of flight, they can also lower it to conserve energy. During the day, they drop their temperatures, lower their metabolism, and enter a state deeper than sleep, called torpor. Some species cope with the decreased food of winter by entering extended torpor, or hibernation. They may drop their temperatures to near freezing and their heart rates to 10 beats per minute. When it is time to wake, their circulatory system warms them to their normal temperature in only 10-20 minutes. This amazing arousal process burns two months' worth of fat reserves, though. Because bats have just enough fat to last through hibernation, disturbing them to arousal can cause them to starve.

Bats' most amazing adaptation, however, may be echolocation, or "seeing" by sound. About 800 species have the ability, which they use for hunting and navigation. The bat emits sound pulses through its mouth or nostrils and uses the echoes to form a detailed picture of its nearby surroundings within a fraction of a second. The system is more precise than any human-made sonar and allows bats to avert wires as thin as a human hair, even in total darkness.

The pulses are high-frequency, typically around 50,000 Hertz (humans cannot detect frequencies above 20,000 Hertz). This is the range necessary for identifying and locating small objects, such as insects. Because different frequencies give different information, bats can, at will, alter their frequencies, even in pattern and complexity. The pulse is produced by forcing air past extra thin, tightly-stretched vocal membranes unique to bats. One species' vocal chords vibrate 105,000 times per second. To avoid deafening itself, the bat must contract a muscle in its ear before each call. Then for the bat to hear the echo, the muscle must relax. Sometimes, this happens 200 times per second.

Our Nighttime Allies

While we sleep, bats are busy helping us. They are essential to controlling night-flying insects that cost farmers and foresters millions of dollars. The Cavern's colony alone consumes four to six thousand pounds of insects each night, about half of it in pests that feed on alfalfa and cotton crops. Bats are a free, self-perpetuating, environmentally safe, highly effective way to control insects — a treasure.

Bats also pollinate plants and disperse their seeds. Almost four hundred commercially important tropical plants depend on bats, including those that produce bananas, avocados, cashews, and tequila. Bats are responsible for seed dispersal and pollination of the new growth in cleared rainforests. In the American Southwest and Northern Mexico, bats pollinate important desert plants. If the bats become endangered, so do these plants and the entire chain of life that depends on them. The ecosystem suffers.

Photo credit—NPS/D. A. Buehler

Each evening from May to October, visitors gather at the Natural Entrance amphitheater to hear a program on bats and witness the emergence of the Cavern's half-million Mexican free-tailed bats as they fly out to hunt insects for the night.

Photo credit—Merlin D. Tuttle

Sixteen species of bats inhabit the park. The pallid bat, shown above, is a unique species because it feeds only on ground-dwelling, flightless insects such as centipedes.

Photo credit—Merlin D. Tuttle

Silver-haired bats have beautiful dark brown coats with hairs tipped white and silver. They hibernate in the park in winter.

Photo credit—Merlin D. Tuttle

The echoes are received by large, megaphone-shaped ears. An ear within the ear, the "tragus" directs the echoes, allowing a bat to line up an object as finely as if it were in the crosshairs of a rifle. When the echo reaches the brain, specialized cells analyze it. Some respond only to the fainter of two sounds, some to echoes from a certain direction or distance. Not surprisingly, echolocation is being studied to discover how the brain processes information and to help develop an orientation system for the blind.

The star of Carlsbad's bat flight, the Mexican free-tailed bat, is found in a wide band across the American Southwest and Mexico. Large summer maternity colonies dwell in caves in Texas, Arizona, and New Mexico. Numbering in the millions, these populations are extremely important because bats born here replenish colonies throughout their range.

Females give birth to a single pup the size of a walnut during late June and early July, usually in the afternoon. Mother begins grooming and feeding her pup immediately. During this time, mother and young build a strong bond and learn each other's scents. As more and more babies are born, the walls become a scene of total commotion, thousands of tiny bodies squirming and squeaking and clinging and crawling over each other, constantly calling for their mothers. The mothers can locate their pups through voice and scent.

Around sunset, the bats head toward the Pecos and Black river valleys 25 miles away, where they hunt insects in the agricultural fields all night. The biggest part of their diet is moths, including the bollworm moth, one of the costliest pests of farmers. Nursing females can eat more than their body weight in insects each night.

Bats in the Belfry and Other Myths

Sure, bats hang out in belfries. They're domes that allow bats to crowd together and stay warm. How this became connected to being crazy, no one seems to know. Humans have created myths that have unfairly depicted and villainized bats.

Consider:

Myth: All bats carry rabies. Truth: Ninety seven percent of human rabies cases worldwide are contracted from unvaccinated dogs. Only one-half of one percent of bats contract it, and they quickly sicken and die. If you can reach a bat, it is probably sick or dead and should not be handled.

Myth: Bats are vampires; they'll suck all your blood out. Truth: There are only three vampire species. They feed mostly on birds and cattle, lapping about one teaspoonful of blood from a sleeping victim, who is rarely bothered enough to awaken. The anticoagulant in vampire saliva is being used to help develop human heart-disease medication.

Myth: Bats are evil and bring bad luck. Truth: The association of bats with evil stems from their nocturnal habits and has no biological basis. Some cultures see the bat as good luck. For example, in China, the bat means good fortune. In one traditional design, it stands for life's five great blessings: health, wealth, good luck, long life, and tranquillity.

Myth: Bats are dingbats. Truth: Bats are intelligent and easily trained. They quickly learn to fly through mazes and act upon either verbal or hand commands. They also learn to recognize and respond to their caretakers, and they aren't blind.

Myth: Bats are dirty. Truth: Bats are exceptionally clean, grooming themselves like cats several times a day. They even clean their teeth with their hind feet claws.

Myth: Bats attack people. Truth: Bats are gentle by nature, not prone to aggression even when chased. They may fly near, but only to catch the bugs around you.

They return to the Cavern toward morning, free falling at speeds of up to 50 miles per hour into the cave's entrance. The bats close their wings, then alternately open them briefly to control speed and direction. This braking action produces the buzz that observers hear. Once inside, mothers feed their babies again. The pups grow fast with their mothers' rich milk and warm roost temperatures of 90-100 degrees Fahrenheit caused by the infants crowding together. These warm temperatures are necessary for the pups to survive.

Photo credit—Merlin D. Tuttle

When the Cavern's Mexican freetails begin to give birth, the cave walls quickly become a scene of total commotion, with thousands of tiny bodies squirming and squeaking. Mothers groom and feed their pups immediately, building strong bonds with them.

At four to five weeks of age, a pup is ready to fly. It lets go of the wall and has 90 feet of airspace between ceiling and ground to master flying on the first try. If it falls to the ground, it dies and will soon be devoured by predators. Fortunately, around 90 percent do succeed and begin to join the nightly hunts. The bat flights then, in late summer, are especially dense, making it a good time to view them.

By mid October, migration gets underway as bats move south toward their winter range in Mexico. They travel in groups, taking advantage of the winds at 10,000 feet. Once in the warmer southern climate, they continue to feed on insects all winter. After mating on their wintering grounds, the bats once again leave for their summer homes, repeating and renewing the cycle of life as they have for thousands of years.

Today, bat populations are declining. Almost half the species in North America are in danger of extinction. Mexican freetails are particularly vulnerable because they occur in large colonies in only a few locations. The biggest cause of decline is intentional killing. In some cases people have exterminated entire colonies.

Equally serious is loss of habitat. In North America, most bats use caves. As human disturbance of cave environments has increased, bats find fewer places to live and are forced to move into less desirable habitat.

Ironically, a third cause of bat decline is pesticides. Because bats are natural predators of insects, pesticides used to kill insects also kill bats. A female eats contaminated insects, then transfers the poison to her baby through her milk. Pesticides such as DDT are stored in a pup's fat until its fat reserves are used for migrating. Then the pesticides are released into the bloodstream. Researchers documented the problem in the 1970s when the Cavern population of Mexican freetails dropped to two hundred thousand. They found up to 40 percent of the Cavern's young bats had received enough of the DDT to kill them. Supposedly safer pesticides have been developed, but researchers suspect they may also have toxic effects.

The good news is that conservation efforts for bats are achieving major successes. Most important is educating people to the beauty and benefits of these gentle creatures, something the park has been doing through its nightly bat flight programs since 1929. Visitors can also join the park's Adopt-A-Bat program, which directly funds education and research on bats. These funds allow park scientists to monitor bat populations and study their biology.

Bats are amazing creatures that are important to the biological diversity of our planet. In the end, whether they survive will be determined by the small conservation efforts each of us makes. We each have the power to help give the night back to our gentle allies, the bats.

It was 5:25 a.m. Ken and I stood at the guard rail of the bat flight amphitheater, peering into the black chasm of the Natural Entrance. We and another couple were the only ones there in the pitch dark.

Suddenly, a bullet whizzed by me — really close — and I instinctively ducked. Then I realized the bullet was a bat. I grinned and nudged Ken. Ken nudged me back as another bat whizzed by, then another and another. Faster and faster the little bat-missiles hurtled in from seemingly all directions in a rain that grew until the air literally sang with the sound of their wings. This was magic completely different from the evening emergence....

Finally, the night yielded, and the bat shower ended. We were joined by the other couple, and as we walked to the parking lot together, we shared our excitement over what we'd just experienced. This couple had had bats in their barn for years and now they wanted to build bat boxes for them outside as soon as they got home to Pennsylvania. In fact, they were leaving today. We said goodbye and watched them lumber off in their RV. The rising sun caught their bumper sticker as they turned onto the road: "Bats need friends."

Bat-friendly Things You Can Do

1. Talk up the truths about bats to your friends; the opportunities to share with people are all around you.

2. Join the Adopt-A-Bat program available in the Cavern Bookstore (http://www.caverns.org).

3. Wear a "Bats need friends" button on your everyday coat. Buy extras and give them away — how about as Halloween trick-or-treats?

4. Encourage your county agricultural extension to institute a bat education program.

5. If your library does not have a book on bats, suggest they purchase one, such as *Bats of Carlsbad Caverns National Park*, available in the Cavern Bookstore. Better yet, buy and donate the book yourself.

6. Put a bat house in your backyard. Prefab houses, as well as plans for building your own, are available from the Cavern Bookstore.

Photo credit—Merlin D. Tuttle

Providing bat houses helps keep bats out of buildings yet preserves these harmless creatures so important to our food crops and environmental health.

The Wild Caves

It was a bright Sunday morning. I was traveling down the highway toward Slaughter Canyon Cave, which isn't a part of the main Cavern, but ranger-guided tours are conducted there throughout the year. Today was to be my first "wild cave" trip. As I turned off onto the canyon road, I thought about what it must have been like to live here, "in the middle of nowhere," when this cave was discovered.

The entrance to Slaughter Canyon Cave is 500 feet up the mountainside, but well worth the hike. Its formations are known throughout the world as some of the finest of their kind, and the cave has a special history to be experienced.

Photo credit—Laurence Parent

Goatherder Tom Tucker found it one day in 1937 when his goats wandered into it. At the time, Tucker was also working as a guano miner in Ogle Cave, on the opposite side of the canyon. The Tuckers lived in the canyon in a little two-room, tin-roofed house and hauled their water by mule from the Harrison homestead at Rattlesnake Springs.

I arrived at the trailhead and started my hike up the canyon to the cave. The flyer had said the walk was a half-mile long with a 500-foot elevation gain. I took the first dozen steps with the enthusiasm of a brand-new caver. The morning was gloriously blue-skied and the trail-side overflowing with flowers, compliments of a recent rain.

Two days after Tucker announced his discovery of his "New Cave," his boss at Ogle Cave slapped a guano mining claim on it, estimating its deposits at 40,000 tons. As it turned out, it held only about one thousand tons of guano, which was too old to be good fertilizer. Although the profits never amounted to anything, mining continued until the 1950s, using tractors and excavation techniques that severely damaged the cave.

Several dozen steps above the canyon floor, the bounce in my step disappeared. This was steep! And I'd thought I was in shape! I'd just started reading Robert Nymeyer's *Carlsbad, Caves, and a Camera*, chronicling his early exploits in this and other wild caves in the park. He'd called this slope a "breath-grabbing haul." I half agreed.

I stopped to rest and enjoy this gorgeous canyon, one of the deeply carved results of the Capitan Reef's erosion. On the east wall, both forereef and backreef are visible. As I turned to resume my climb, flute music floated through the canyon. I looked for the Pan who was playing it and finally saw him, an antlike figure far below on the canyon floor, strolling up the ribbon of sand that marked a dry streambed. What a comfort for a hard walk his music was! It followed me, too, for Pan walked up the trail behind me.

At the mouth of the cave, most of my fellow adventurers were sitting on the rocks waiting for the ranger. Then Pan showed up. "It was you we heard!" we all cried, when his silver flute flashed in the sun. He smiled, confessed, and sat down on a rock to join us.

Photo credit—Urs Widmer

Ranger Paula Carrington came up the trail, and our adventure officially began. Paula unlocked the heavy iron gate covering the mouth of the cave, and I took my first steps into a cave. The air felt cool and damp, a shocking change from the heat outside. It smelled musty. Water dripped in the distance. We were quiet as we descended down the steep entrance and into the dim twilight zone,

Left-hand Tunnel offers visitors an easy walking trip into a portion of the Cavern still in its natural state. The different parts of the old reef are visible as the tunnel trail winds downward.

the zone where natural light can still penetrate. Our flashlights blinked on one by one, their circles of light bobbing here and there as we walked. Even with these, it was spooky, with total darkness always just beyond the reach of the light. At a huge column, the Pillar of Hercules, Paula told us to turn around and say goodbye to the light of day, now a mere dot in the distance. The pillar marked our passage into total darkness.

Once in the dark zone, we swung to the right, passing remnants from the miners. Their digging had left large scars on the floors and walls, still visible. Explorers searching for other treasure dealt more kindly with the cave. In the 1940s and 1950s, expeditions discovered pottery and tools of primitive man, the bones of a Pleistocene camel, and bat bones identified as belonging to an extinct Pleistocene species never seen before. Similar to our modern Mexican free-tailed bats, these Constantine's free-tailed bats deposited guano here for thousands of years until they deserted the cave more than 28,000 years ago.

We passed the Chinese Wall, a snakelike wall 4-1/2 inches high that wanders across the floor for yards. Speleologist Donald Black proposed in 1956 that it be considered a new type of rimstone dam. These dams form when water flows slowly and continuously over an expanse, such as a floor. Where there is an irregularity, the water becomes turbulent and deposits calcite, eventually forming a ridge that grows into a dam. The Chinese Wall posed questions for Black, though, because it's so highly furled, like ribbon taffy. He called it a furled rimstone dam.

We came to one of the cave's most unusual and famous formations, the Klansman, which may be the scariest speleothem in the world. An old, brown stalagmite has been covered by white flowstone growing over it like a shroud. The Klansman is actually a formation called a bell canopy, but to Nymeyer it was simply a monster, crouched and daring him to pass. He wrote, "It took no strong imagination to see an evil, bestial face leering out from beneath the hood, the broad, ugly mouth filled with yellow, straggly teeth...."

We sneaked past it and entered the Christmas Tree Room, which had left Nymeyer speechless and had the same effect on me. He wrote, "...the walls were buried behind a maze of colorful flowstone waterfalls, great hanging masses of stone draperies, delicately tapered stalactites, mounds and protuberances and niches." To me it was a roomful of white cake frosting. In the center sat the 39-foot-tall Christmas Tree, a bell canopy like the Klansman, but as far away from it in appearance as angels are from devils. The tree's olive green stone "branches" drooped under the weight of a sparkling mantle of "snow" made of millions of tiny calcite crystals. Paula said this blanket sparkles only when the formation is dry and inactive, as it was now. Other formations in the room were active, however. To prove it, Paula had us turn out our lights, and we listened to them grow. Drip, drip, plunk.

We went from here to the Monarch Room, graced by the 89-foot-tall Monarch, one of the largest formations in the park. Paula suggested we have another blackout, because this room was inactive and should sound different in the dark than the Christmas Tree Room. The lights went out. The silence was so complete it was almost unbearable. Suddenly, Pan began to play. His crystalline notes brought the darkness to life.

When we turned the lights on, the peace of the music seemed to have filled the cave, so it was especially jarring to move on to the guano pits where the miners had thoughtlessly cut and quarried. The pits were as deep as we were tall. From the guano walls, the ancient bat bones stuck out, many as delicate as toothpicks. I stood amongst them, letting the group go ahead. Odd feelings overcame me, as if I was peering into something very old and hidden. I shivered and hurried along. On the other side, our tour was ending. Paula was explaining the cave's biggest mystery was the wall of rare Indian pictographs in the alcove to our right, rare because this was the dark zone, a zone in caves where pictographs are almost never found.

Once outside, I practically ran down the trail and headed for the park's visitor center. I was now "into" wild caving, by golly, and I had to go to the Hall of the White Giant, destination of one of the park's most challenging off-trail trips. Soon, I was set to go the morning of my last day in the park. It would be a fitting climax to my visit.

Meanwhile, Ken and I took the Lower Cave tour. It's among the easiest of the wild cave trips and gives you just a hint of what caving is about. Led by rangers Dave Elkowitz and Paula Carrington, the trip started by suiting up in hard hats and climbing down a ladder from the Big Room. At the bottom, we had to ease down a slope of smooth flowstone to get to the main part of Lower Cave. Thankfully, nobody fell.

Willis T. Lee visited Lower Cave on his 1924 expedition and now we went to one of the areas he saw, the Rookery. His son, Dana, who was on the trip, wrote, "They found a very beautiful part of the cave.... There are bushels of little round stones, like marbles. They are from an inch in diameter to the size of small shot. They are found in little drip cups, and resemble eggs in a nest." What Dana described were cave pearls, which form when water drips into a pool, splashing loose bits of matter, such as sand grains, rolling them around and coating them evenly with successive layers of calcite. They're about the size of real pearls, and the water gives them a similar patina.

Just past the Rookery, we had to pick our way through an area of trickling water. Dave led the way safely, but I jumped over what seemed to be the smallest rivulet. As my foot came in for a landing, it hit wet flowstone just long enough to prepare me for the coming crash between my bottom and the stone. Ouch! Dave applied bandaids to my bleeding elbow. I was now an initiated (and humbled) caver. Flowstone, by the way, forms when water flows in thin films over a large surface, depositing layer upon layer of calcite. Often colored by other minerals, it takes a variety of forms, from frozen waterfalls and cascades to thick sheets on the floor, such as my bottom had just discovered.

We passed a rimstone dam. Feeling like a veteran from my Slaughter Canyon trip, I casually said to Ken, "Oh, there's a rimstone dam." "A what?" he asked. I explained. These dams generally grow on slopes. The greater the slope, the higher the dam; the highest ones in the world are 45 feet high. What Black didn't know that made him wonder about the Chinese Wall is that dams become tightly furled when they're on low slopes.

We visited the Colonel Boles Room, where the superintendent loved to take celebrities. Finding an alcove, we all sat down. Dave reached behind a loose rock, and pulled out a logbook. We were each to sign our names and comments for posterity to read. I couldn't think of anything profound or elegant to write under "Comments," so I left an inside joke. I wrote, "Nice, hard flowstone." After signing the log, we turned off our lights to experience the cave in its natural state. Endless seconds of silence and darkness.

When Slaughter Canyon Cave was first discovered, the owner heralded it as being larger than Carlsbad Cavern. That proved false, but it did open up to show explorers some of the most beautiful and unusual of the park's cave formations. From top to bottom: the Chinese Wall, Klansman, Christmas Tree, and Teardrop.

Finally, Ken broke the mood. "I know these speleothems grow in the dark," he said, "but it doesn't make sense." Laughing at his own question he continued, "How do the water drops know where to go?"

"That's a good point," Dave answered. "We humans are so light-oriented we can't comprehend endless darkness." When the blackout ended, it was time to get back up the long expanse of flowstone and the ladder, which I did just fine. This caving stuff was great.

As Paula and I kept bumping into one another at the park, I decided to take another trip with her to Slaughter Canyon Cave to see the wall of pictographs. These prehistoric drawings are some of the few examples of deep cave art north of Mexico. Ken came too. The flowers along the trail were even more profuse than they had been a few days before. Mallow covered the slope like pink snow. Yellow blossoms of every size and shape grew out of the cracks in the rocks.

We took Ken to see the guano pits first. This time, I felt only sorrow as I looked at the deeply excavated earth with the broken-toothpick bat bones sticking out of the cuts. I thought of the destruction done in the quest for profits. And no profits were ever gained.

The little chamber with the pictographs was nearby, just big enough for the three of us. The minute I entered, I felt I was stepping on sacred ground. A small pool filled most of the floor. Water dripped into it leisurely from above. Unlike the guano pits, this was a place of peace. Paula pointed out the pictographs. They were all about chest height, drawn in yellow, red, and blue-black paint. Some were so faded you had to squint to see them. They were arranged across the wall in what seemed to be separate pictures of different experiences. One of long, parallel zigzag lines intrigued us all. As we stood there, I imagined the area centuries ago, the artists coming here to rest, draw water, reflect, and paint. What grand or simple thoughts inspired them? I felt honored to be glimpsing their world.

We left, and as I neared the mouth of the cave, a single drop of water fell from the ceiling onto my cheek. Paula said it was a cave kiss, and it meant the cave wanted me to come back. I'd get two more kisses — from the Cavern — before I departed the park.

The next day, we toured Left-hand Tunnel. It's an easy walking trip and a great geology lesson. You move from the Capitan Reef to the forereef and see wonderful fossil rocks along the way. At the end of Left-hand Tunnel, far beyond the end of our tour, Lake of the Clouds marks the deepest point in the Cavern, 1,037 feet below the entrance. Here and in two adjoining rooms, more than one hundred fringed myotis bats raise their young each summer.

Photo credit—Urs Widmer

Some wild cave areas need to remain pristine for the benefit of the cave ecosystem and its wildlife. Lake of the Clouds, at the end of Left-hand Tunnel in Carlsbad Cavern, is home to a small colony of fringed myotis bats and is accessible only to researchers.

Chapter 6 ◆ Wild Caves

Dr. Ken Geluso and Troy Best have been studying them to determine how they leave the Cavern — through the Natural Entrance, which is about 1-1/4 miles away and is a long, energy-expensive flight, or via some unknown shortcut to the Bat Cave entrance. With Adopt-A-Bat program funding, Geluso and Best fitted 13 bats with tiny radio transmitters and radiotracked them to see where they went each night. They found that the fringed myotis do take the long way out of the Cavern, flying up the Main Corridor and out the big Natural Entrance, right along with the Mexican free-tailed bats. Geluso thinks the fringed myotis roost in the deepest part of the cave because it's the warmest. Remember, temperatures must be warm for pups to grow. Because there aren't enough fringed myotis to raise the temperature by clustering, as the thousands of Mexican freetails do, they instead pick the warmest spot in the cave.

That night I tossed and turned and dreamed of getting stuck in narrow tunnels. The reason was no mystery to me. My trip to the Hall of the White Giant, which my ranger guides told me would include crawling through tight places, was scheduled for the next morning. It had been years since I'd wriggled through skinny lava tubes at home in Northern California, and as I'd gotten older, I'd developed some phobias. Despite the fact that I'm not fearful of new experiences, I worried that I'd freak out with tons of rock pressing in on me.

Early next morning, I pulled on my oldest jeans and red wolf sweatshirt, gulped a cup of coffee, and took off for the park. By the time I met my guides, Dave Elkowitz and Robert Power, in the equipment room, I had given myself a full-blown case of fear. As we suited up with knee pads, elbow pads, and hard hats, I confessed my state to Dave. He treated it more like a molehill than the mountain I'd made it. "Just don't fight the cave," he said. "Meet it on its terms, not yours, and you'll do fine."

Padded and armed with lights, we took the elevator to the Big Room and then walked up the Main Corridor. Halfway, Dave stopped at a little hole that reminded me of the one in *Alice in Wonderland*. "Here we are," he said. "We're going in there?" I asked. "Yep," Dave said, taking off his daypack because he said he wouldn't be able to get through the entrance with it on. He'd push it ahead of him through these initial crawls.

I followed him into the hole, finding myself immediately in a labyrinth that twisted and dipped and rose like a fun-house tunnel. I found myself inch-worming forward on my tummy. It wasn't tight, just comfortable, and I began to relax. Hey, this was fun!

But then we reached Matlock's Pinch, named for the ranger who first "negotiated" it, as cavers say, and it does deserve that term. As I entered it, Dave, just ahead of me, began giving me almost foot-by-foot instructions as to how best to move forward. I followed them to the letter. In places I had to twist several ways before finding one that worked. Dave encouraged me from ahead, Robert from behind, but just when I thought the pinch was as small as it could get, it seemed to shrink. I panicked. I had to get out of here now, but I couldn't even move.

The White Giant, a domed stalagmite, maintains a commanding presence over the Hall of the White Giant. The trip to get here offers some of the park's most challenging and rewarding wild caving.

Then I remembered what Dave had said. "Don't fight the cave," and the panic subsided. I felt my body in contact with the cool, smooth rock, and where a moment ago I felt the cave walls would crush me, now they embraced me. I put my cheek down on the floor. This was my Mother Earth, and I let go to her. Finally, I moved on. I scraped my elbow. The mud on the floor ground into my clothes. It didn't matter. I was at home here.

Just past the pinch, I had my first chance to "chimney," a technique that looks just like it sounds. With one foot on one wall, the other on the opposite wall, you haul yourself up an open space using whatever handholds and footholds you can find. As a short person, I had a disadvantage, and yet I surprised myself with my ability. I was so proud when I reached the top. Then I stood up and banged my head. Glad I wore a hard hat!

Now we walked along the plain, sandy-floored Sand Passage, a high, wide joint in the dolomite beds of the backreef. How different it looked from the ornately decorated rooms of the main reef. As we moved toward the main reef, small formations began to appear. Dave discovered delicate angel's hair crystals. A little further, we came upon a group of miniature stalagmites. Their shapes and arrangement made them look to me exactly like a Christmas nativity crèche, complete with plump, white sheep.

Even with the increasing decorations hinting that we were nearing our destination, I was brought up short when we reached the hall. Dave gestured toward its yawning entrance. "The Giant is in there," he said, and swept his flashlight over the pitch black cavern, giving me flickering glimpses of white shapes in the dark. He held the light on the Giant. "There it is," he whispered. It was a giant, sitting by itself at the top of a hill of silt, like a king upon his throne. It commanded the large hall with such a presence that I half expected it to speak, wanting to know why we were here.

We climbed up the hill for a closer view. This giant domed stalagmite truly sits alone. The ceiling of the hall is covered with soda straws, but curiously, none grows above the Giant. Across the hall a flowstone waterfall froths in red, peach, and brown. What a kingdom for a giant to rule. What a reward to reap for the work to get here.

We stayed awhile, marveling, then left and found a resting spot for a blackout. A single *longipes* cave cricket sat on the floor near us. Dave picked it up gently and placed it in a nook. "There you go, guy," he said, "out of harm's way." The lights went off, and we told ghost stories. When our lights went back on, the cricket hadn't moved a millimeter. I wondered if it was demonstrating for us the thrifty way that creatures in the food-poor cave environment conserve their energy.

Our spirits high, we began our return. Along the way, both rangers were already encouraging me to come back to the park for more caving. There's Spider Cave to do, Dave said, a completely different kind of wild cave than this, and there are eight backcountry caves accessible by permit for those who are qualified.

In what seemed no time at all we were at Matlock's Pinch. This time I took it like an old pro. A few minutes later, we emerged, back-ends first, into the Main Corridor from the same little hole that had led us in. To say the least, we surprised passersby. We were dirty and happy and joked all the way to the elevator.

Back in the equipment room, I stripped off my gear and replaced it on the shelves with affection. I thanked Dave and Robert, and we parted with the hearty handshakes of friends. I walked through the visitor center a different woman than I'd been a few hours before. Cavers talk about pushing the leads in a cave to discover new passages. I had pushed my own "inner leads" on this trip and had grown a little larger. Yes, I'll come back to do Spider. Then there are those permit caves...

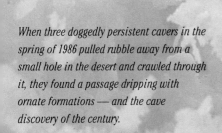

The Lechuguilla Treasure
chapter seven

*I*t was Memorial Day weekend, 1986. Three cavers stood at the slit-like entrance to Lechuguilla Cave four miles from Carlsbad Cavern, waiting in the warming desert day for three other cavers. This dig was a six-person job, but it had been burning people out; not many wanted to spend a holiday weekend digging in a hole that seemed to be going nowhere, despite the volumes of air that blew from between the rocks at times. Cavers have a saying for discovering caves: "If it blows, it goes." But this one hadn't gone.

The leader, Dave Allured, finally tired of waiting for the others and suggested that the three of them go to work. They rappelled down the 90-foot entrance and began digging through the rubble, uncovering a small hole that drew air in so strongly it sucked in the dirt as fast as they dug it out. The hole just kept expanding. When it stopped, one of the cavers, Rick Bridges, poked his hand down it. The rock was only three or four inches thick. The cavers quickly dug that out of the way and created a hole big enough to crawl through. Shortly they found themselves standing in a passage dripping with formations. Little did they know that they had just made what cavers and scientists alike would describe as the biggest cave discovery of this century.

Lechuguilla had been known about since 1914, when it was mined for a short time for guano. Later, a few cavers investigated its two hundred feet of passage, which ended in a pile of rock rubble. They nicknamed it Misery Hole and described it as "small and somewhat disappointing." In the 1970s, then again in early 1984, groups of cavers began digging. There were four trips over the next two years, burning out cavers with the hard, no-glory work until that 25th day of May 1986, when only three could be found to dig.

By the end of breakthrough week, Allured's team had mapped 3,510 feet to a depth of 702 feet. A month later a geologic team confirmed that if a downward southerly direction were followed, the Capitan Reef would be entered, where large passages — possibly exceeding Carlsbad Cavern's in size — could be expected. The NPS immediately drew up a management plan for the cave. Meanwhile the Lechuguilla Cave Project was organized and began investigation of the cave in August of 1987.

When three doggedly persistent cavers in the spring of 1986 pulled rubble away from a small hole in the desert and crawled through it, they found a passage dripping with ornate formations — and the cave discovery of the century.

Photo credit—NPS/Bosted

For the next two years, project cavers explored and surveyed in a frenzy, almost doubling the length and depth of the cave each expedition. By summer of 1989, cavers from seven nations had volunteered thousands of hours in the cave. Today the surveyed passage length stands at over one hundred miles, more than triple that of Carlsbad Cavern, making it the third longest cave in the U.S. Evidence suggests that it may be a lot longer.

Exploring a big cave calls for coordination. Lechuguilla's explorers developed a system of tag-team caving, by which one team would enter the cave as the other came out, taking up where they left off. Teams would be in the cave for up to 36 hours, exploring until sleepiness overcame them. Then they would find a flat area big enough for a body, wrap up in a plastic garbage bag to stay warm in the 99+ percent humidity, and sleep a few hours. Up top, notes and sketches would be input to a computer and progress plotted.

It was hard work. On the March 1988 expedition, Pat Kambesis wrote, "My canteen held barely a swallow. All of my provisions were gone. My neck ached from hours spent hunched over the survey book, and I had writer's cramp. Gypsum sand had worked its way into my pack straps, causing nasty abrasions on my shoulders. The cave kept going. I couldn't."

The way forward challenged body and mind. Squeezes lined with popcorn scratched arms and legs. And always there was punishing heat. Lechuguilla is a warm cave — 68 degrees Fahrenheit With high humidity as well, the minute you move, you sweat. There is also real danger to contend with, hinted at by names like Freak-Out Traverse, where a caver must cross a hundred-foot pit on a narrow ledge, at one point with only a big rock to hold onto. The night it was named, the rock moved while a caver was holding onto it.

Another freak-out occurred during the March 1988 expedition. The team had just discovered the Chandelier Graveyard and stopped to rest. Caver Steve Davis wandered into the boneyard that formed the walls to check out a tunnel. Within minutes he popped out into what he thought was the room he'd just left, disappointed the tunnel went nowhere. Then he looked around. No teammates. This was a different room. He turned to find the way out, but the dozens of holes in the wall all looked the same. Davis was nervous — he had no food or water. But he did have surveyor's tape, so he began to check each hole for the way back, systematically marking with tape as he went. Five and a half hours later he emerged on a balcony 30 feet above the Chandelier Graveyard. His relieved teammates tossed him a rope, and he descended. A bonus for the team was that the boneyard led to discovery of a mile of virgin cave.

The danger and exhausting work were all quickly forgotten each time the cave opened up to something like the Chandelier Ballroom. One member of the team that discovered it in January 1988, Pat Kambesis, wrote, "In the distance we could see strange shapes hanging from the ceiling, any-where from five to twelve feet long. These stalks were gypsum and at the ends were huge sprays of selenite crystals...Just one of these would be the showcase of any cave — here were groves of them!...this was a world-class occurrence." Some of the chandeliers turned out to be 20 feet long, the largest in the world.

The intensity of decoration in Lechuguilla is, according to Kambesis, "nerve-wracking." The rarity, size, and diversity of its features is singular in the world. For example, helictites are twisting forma-tions that grow from cave walls and have been described as looking like spaghetti or "the horrible, snaky tresses of Medusa." But until they were discovered growing from Lechuguilla's pool walls, *subaqueous* helictites were never even imagined. These underwater formations are created when water containing dissolved gypsum enters a carbonate-rich pool. The mixing of the water causes a ring of calcium carbonate to be deposited. Water continues to seep through this ring, and a lengthening helictite with a tiny central canal is created. Impurities cause them to twist.

Gypsum, found rarely and in small amounts in other caves, is everywhere in Lechuguilla. Cavers have described gypsum blocks as big as an upended bus and gypsum-lined passages as looking like "the inside of a powdered sugar donut." Native sulfur, also rare in caves, is found in large blocks in Lechuguilla.

Hydromagnesite balloons, rare in the world, occur in greater numbers than in any other known cave. Formations that look like inflated balloons or satiny freshwater pearls, they're fragile and short-lived. Some observed in Carlsbad Cavern dried, cracked, and deflated in just eight years.

Brilliant white aragonite grows throughout the cave. Its crystals are clusters of sharp needles resembling thistles. Often called "frostwork," it's found on walls, ceilings, and sometimes on floors, where it forms "bushes." Many places in the cave are encrusted with bushes up to 4-1/2 feet tall, some of the most impressive of such displays ever seen.

Folia, rare formations that look like folded rock, coat the walls and ceilings for the last hundred feet leading to the deepest point of the cave. Formed by water-level fluctuations, researchers think they may hold records of past water conditions in the cave.

On the April 1989 expedition, geologist Kiym Cunningham went down to the deepest known pool in the cave, 1,501 feet underground, to check it for hydrogen sulfide. Cavers had thought they smelled the distinctive rotten-egg odor there. This could mean they were nearing the water table, which would be a first for a Guadalupe cave. Now, Cunningham submerged his hands into the pool and felt a piece of loose rock. He brought it out, an old piece of folia, and took it back to his lab to see what some areas of unusual staining were.

After peering at the stains under the microscope for several hours, he saw fungi, which feed on bacteria. Amazed, he looked closer and found what he thought were bacterial filaments. He stared at them, mystified. How could something be living so deep with no organic food? He went back to the cave, looking for a food source, and started thinking about rock-eating bacteria, called chemolithotrophs. They existed in deep aquifers, where they form the basis of rich microbial ecosystems. Were they here as well? The implication was mind-boggling. Scientists have discovered a strong connection between biology and geology, and nowhere is it stronger than in limestone, for limestone has biological sources and continues to have biological activity.

Now, Cunningham looked for the bacterias' source of energy in the "weird things" cavers had been finding. He started with corrosion residue, a mud-like substance the consistency of moist graphite, which hung from ceilings and walls throughout the cave. The material was so fine, though, that time after time his lab process would blow it away before he could get a look at it. Determined, he finally succeeded one night and was astounded at what he saw: dense populations of bacteria jutting out of crystals everywhere, as if the two had come together purposely.

Not a microbiologist himself, Cunningham consulted one of the best, David Updegraff, who told him that he had a phenomenon of planetary importance and guided him forward. Cunningham finally hypothesized that the bacteria were eating rock. He also began studying the cave's other "weird things," which looked not like rocks but like calcite-encrusted, fossilized bacterial filaments, and that is what they turned out to be. Cunningham coined the term "biothem" to describe them.

The biothems brought him to two more amazing realizations. First, that bacteria lived throughout the cave. Second, that the bacteria in the cave today are the descendants of those sulfur-loving ones in the oil fields when the cave was formed. That means Lechuguilla is a living relic of an ancient underground ecosystem, protected through millennia because of its exceptional isolation from the surface. Not only did the small, rubble-strewn entrance keep the cave virtually closed, a siltstone caprock over the area also diverted surface water that would have — and did, in Carlsbad Cavern — wash out much of the cave's sulfur and gypsum. Instead, Cunningham says, "Lechuguilla is an incredibly preserved sulfate paradise. An incredibly precious one."

When Cunningham began making his discoveries, cave ecologist Diana Northup was studying the cave's invertebrates. The discovery of fungi on the folia piqued her interest. Here was evidence that microbial life teemed more than a thousand feet under the surface. She began working to isolate fungi and bacteria and found a few dozen kinds in low numbers. This was consistent, she wrote, with the low-nutrient environment of a cave.

Northup presented her findings at a meeting also attended by microbiologist Larry Mallory. As Mallory listened to her, sirens sounded in his head, because he had just found over a hundred kinds of bacteria in Mammoth Cave. He had developed techniques to culture cave microbes on the low-nutrient diet they were used to rather than the "fat turkey sandwiches" of traditional techniques, which killed them. He knew he could find more kinds of bacteria in Lechuguilla. He approached Northup and a trip was set.

What was once considered a small cave, only 200 feet in length, has now been explored to a length of more than 100 miles; it is the world's fifth longest cave. While its spectacular features have attracted world-wide attention, the cave's fragile nature and pristine environment have challenged the best management and protection strategies of the National Park Service. Lechuguilla Cave is a jewel, comparable in beauty and importance to the best at Yosemite, Yellowstone, Grand Canyon or Sequoia national parks. Whether visitors see it in person or not, we are all richer because it is there.

Exploring cavers in Lechuguilla forgot the exhausting work of pushing leads each time they made a world class discovery like the Chandelier Ballroom. It is filled with groves of gypsum chandeliers from five to twenty feet long — the largest ever found.

Photo credit—NPS/Dave Bunnell

After this first trip, Mallory and Northup began working together regularly in the cave, discovering hundreds of taxa of bacteria — most of them unknowns — in its pools. Soon, James Bigelow at the Vermont Cancer Center called, wanting to know if Mallory had screened his bacteria for anti-cancer activity. Mallory said no, he had honestly never thought of it. Bigelow asked, "Do you want to do it? We'll pay." Mallory said yes.

A week later he drove a "chicken soup" of 10 organisms up to Vermont. Three weeks later Bigelow called to tell him 50 percent had come back significantly toxic to cancer cells, and three of those had come back at serum level — the level of a finished drug. Astonished, Mallory looked to see which bacteria they were. They were unknowns.

Mallory explains that caves hold promise for natural disease-fighting products. The long periods of stable conditions and a nutrient-poor environment cause bacteria to develop strong reactions — an attitude of "Invade my pool and you're lunch." This reaction could make these bacteria good cancer-fighting agents. Since the initial discovery, a steady 30 percent of Mallory's bacteria show significant activity against disease, and the anti-cancer agent is in product development. Northup is cataloging the finds by their DNA and looking for beneficial fungi. She has isolated nearly one hundred strains and expects to find many more. Best of all, Mallory is finding each pool has a different community of microbes. He says Lechuguilla has as much microbial diversity as the rainforest and is as rich with microbial life as surface soil. The significance, he says, is "new bugs, new drugs."

While Mallory, Northup, and Cunningham were studying microbes, a NASA team was looking for ways to find out about life on Mars. A recent paper had described a hypothetical Martian ecosystem in which microbes used the large amounts of sulfur in the planet's soil for energy. When one of the scientists heard about Lechuguilla being sulfur rich, he realized it might be a model for Mars. The team went to find out in 1994 and, like Cunningham, found treasure in the corrosion residue.

Brilliant white, frostlike aragonite grows on walls, ceilings, and floors throughout Lechuguilla. Many places are encrusted with aragonite "bushes" up to 4-1/2 feet tall, some of the most impressive of such displays ever seen in a cave.

Photo credit—NPS/John Brooks

Team member Penny Boston says it captured her attention instantly. "It's very fluffy, because the mass of rock has been lost. It forms in fabulous colors from lemon yellow to salmon pink to screaming yellow-orange to chestnut brown and dark brown. It's a feast for the eyes." She says it accumulates where there are updrafts of air, hanging in shaggy bits in some places and forming thick coatings in others.

Everyone studying the corrosion residue is still stroking their chins over it. All agree that it is a jungle of microbes, but what they are doing is not definitive. Boston says the bacteria are crumbling the rock, but she does not yet know if they're eating it or if the corrosion residue is just a by-product of their metabolisms. Her intuition tells her she is seeing the weathering of rock by microbes, the same process we see as soil-building on the earth's surface. She agrees with Cunningham, who now thinks the bacteria are being fed by minerals, gases, and possibly even organic matter in the air.

Meanwhile, scientists are studying the connection between microbes and cave-forming processes, a concept known as "biomineralization." As it turns out, bacteria and fungi not only act as "nuclei" for crystals, as in the formation of biothems, but they also play a part in the growth and erosion of speleothems and even affect which mineral is deposited.

Also important, a mineral survey headed by geologist Harvey DuChene is yielding a map of Lechuguilla's features. Although DuChene is using it to locate the "geologically rare, significant, and highly fragile," he says his system can be used to map any aspect of the cave. DuChene's long-term goal is to map all the Guadalupe caves, allowing one to see the geological picture from one end of the mountains to the other. He has mapped at four thousand points in Lechuguilla. Special finds include tyuyamunite, a uranium mineral; bright yellow elemental sulfur; bright green fluorapatite; and sky blue celestite.

There are threats to this incredible treasure. Even with good management and what NPS cave specialist Ron Kerbo has called the "most caring, loving, careful exploration" of any cave he has been in, Lechuguilla is being impacted by people. Northup is studying these impacts and finding one of the biggest threats to be the carbon we introduced by the hair, lint, and tens of thousands of skin fragments we shed each minute. This carbon buildup makes the environment unlivable for native bacteria. The solution may be to give the cave periodic rests from people. Microclimatologist John McLean says we could be affecting the cave's climate as well, causing changes that could alter pool ecosystems and formations. McLean is working to establish a baseline of information about the cave's current climate so changes can be measured over time.

Perhaps the greatest threats to Lechuguilla, however, are political. When Lechuguilla was discovered, local business people pushed to commercialize the cave. Proponents brought in a consultant, who assessed the cave and concluded the cost and damage caused in development would be too great to make the venture profitable.

Another major struggle occurred over oil and gas drilling on Bureau of Land Management (BLM) land just outside the park. Exploration was scheduled to begin two thousand feet from the known cave. Because drilling could breach a passage, the NPS joined with other groups to stop the action. The result was the 1993 Lechuguilla Cave Protection Act, which created a protection zone adjacent to the cave's entrance where drilling was not allowed.

Oil and gas geologists maintain there is a level of danger. There have been drilling breaches in the area, one so large it took semi-trailers full of gravel to plug. Pouring concrete over Lechuguilla's treasures is bad enough, but an even worse danger is poisonous gases. The cave systems in the area have been shown to be interconnected. Thus, if a passage is breached, gases from the well bore could be released into Lechuguilla. In addition to altering the cave's ecosystem, the gases could kill people.

The threats to Lechuguilla parallel those looming over the treasures in all of our national parks. As the National Parks and Conservation Association points out, our society has little heritage and is destroying what it has for the sake of economic profit. Poll after poll shows that we Americans love our parks and are willing to support them.

The key is to think globally and act locally. Look around you. How can you speak out? Where can you volunteer? As anthropologist Margaret Meade once said, "Never doubt that a group of thoughtful, committed citizens can change the world. Indeed, it's the only thing that ever has."